PLAY THERAPY
A Strategic Approach

PLAY THERAPY
A Strategic Approach

By

STANLEY KISSEL, PH.D.
Rochester, New York

CHARLES C THOMAS • PUBLISHER
Springfield • Illinois • U.S.A.

Published and Distributed Throughout the World by

CHARLES C THOMAS • PUBLISHER
2600 South First Street
Springfield, Illinois 62794-9265

This book is protected by copyright. No part of
it may be reproduced in any manner without
written permission from the publisher.

© *1990 by* CHARLES C THOMAS • PUBLISHER

ISBN 0-398-05708-7

Library of Congress Catalog Card Number: 90-11137

With THOMAS BOOKS *careful attention is given to all details of manufacturing and design. It is the Publisher's desire to present books that are satisfactory as to their physical qualities and artistic possibilities and appropriate for their particular use.* THOMAS BOOKS *will be true to those laws of quality that assure a good name and good will.*

Printed in the United States of America
SC-R-3

Library of Congress Cataloging-in-Publication Data

Kissel, Stanley.
    Play therapy : a strategic approach / by Stanley Kissel.
      p. cm.
    Includes bibliographical references.
    Includes index.
    ISBN 0-398-05708-7
    1. Play therapy. I. Title.
    [DNLM: 1. Play Therapy—in infancy & childhood. 2. Play Therapy—methods. WS 350.2 K61p]
RJ505.P6K48 1990
618.92'891653—dc20
DLC
for Library of Congress   90-11137
                                                                           CIP

*Dedicated with Love
to the memory of
Elizabeth Ann Kissel
Steven Michael Kissel
and to the life of
Neal Kissel
Pearl Kissel*

PREFACE

More and more children are showing dysfunctional reactions and are having greater difficulties learning in school. Academic difficulties, behavior problems, and an inability to relate to authority figures are at times the result of emotional difficulties and at other times the cause. It makes little difference if a child's problems stem from sociocultural differences, education-based deficiencies, or fractured families, because whatever their origins they leave scars which impact a child's self-esteem.

The decades of the seventies and eighties emphasized family-oriented intervention strategies with major emphasis placed on family unit psychotherapy. As clinicians gained greater experience working with multiple populations in a family therapy intervention, they discovered deficiencies in their skills and knowledge about working with children. Individually-oriented play therapy seems to be making a popular resurgence as witnessed by the publications of a number of edited volumes. For the most part these have been technique-oriented and have emphasized the importance of matching technique to children rather than having children conform to a therapist's particular theoretical persuasion. The author is committed to that point of view.

The present volume will provide the reader with a more integrated approach to working with children rather than a narrow technique-oriented one. However, the reader will have sufficient latitude so he or she can integrate his or her current practice with the points of view presented. Play therapy from a strategic provides the clinician of the 1990s a broad-based eclectic orientation to better equip them to work with troubled or troublesome children.

Play Therapy will initially review for the reader some of the key antecedents of the renaissance of play therapy and then lay the theoretical foundation for working with children using play in addition to/or as a supplement to talk intervention. Illustrations and commentaries regarding the multiple roles the therapist plays while engaging the child will orient and instruct the psychotherapist to working with children, and finally the therapist will be taught to make meaningful contact with the child initially and during the different phases of psychotherapy. Indications for termination of therapy will conclude the work.

ACKNOWLEDGMENTS

I would like to publicly express my appreciation to some of my teachers and colleagues who helped me to learn about children and to appreciate the complexities of engaging children in the playroom. Sheppard Goldberg helped me to understand the value of a clinical approach when I was surrounded by academics; Jack Reisman taught me there was more to a reflection than saying "you feel . . . "; David Elkind guided me through the murky waters of Piaget's Developmental Theory and clarified its social and clinical implications; and Werner Halpern, friend, collaborator, and mentor, taught me about menshkeit.

Peter A. Keller, Senior Editor of the *Innovations in Clinical Practice: A Source Book* was extremely helpful when I developed some of the techniques which appear in Chapter 5 and first appeared as separate articles in *Innovations in Clinical Psychology: A Source Book.*

I am grateful to Charles Kantor for his contributions to the original conception of this approach to play therapy.

For typing the manuscript I am indebted to Nancy Giorgione.

CONTENTS

	Page
Preface	vii

Chapter

1. Pathways to Play Therapy 3
2. Before Entering the Playroom: Theoretical Foundations 11
3. Arriving at the Door: The Role of the Play Therapist 23
4. Talking With Children in the Playroom: Mirroring 31
5. Playing With Children in the Playroom: Maneuvering 37
6. Beginnings and Endings of Play Therapy: Tempo 77
   References 89
   Index 93

PLAY THERAPY
A Strategic Approach

Chapter 1

PATHWAYS TO PLAY THERAPY

In the beginning, mental health Intervention tactics were routed in religious and mystical practices. Deviant or "strange" behavior was looked upon as the work of the devil—banishment, sequestering, or death were the treatment tactics of choice. Advances in the biological sciences during the nineteenth century led to changing views of mental illness and its cures. However, the pioneering work of Freud which placed important emphasis on unconscious mental processes as a major factor to understanding irrational actions, disturbed thoughts, and symptoms of emotional illness created revolutionary changes in the treatment of disturbed individuals. Unfortunately, these advanced, more humanistic treatment approaches were not initially afforded to children.

An unprecedented interest in children and their development has come to dominate the twentieth century. The rise of the affluent middle class, of urbanization, of longevity, of technology, and of leisure are among factors that converged to give the child a new status in society. Preparation for the adult role became a paramount concern and it was not surprising at the turn of the century that special attention was being focused on children, handicapped and normal (Reisman, 1966; Halpern and Kissel, 1976.)

Clinicians took as their lead the pioneering work of Sigmund Freud. Freud's serminal contribution to child therapy was the analysis of a five-year-old phobic carried out through correspondence with the child's father and without benefit of direct observation.

In the mid-twentieth century child therapy, like its adult counterpart, was dominated by psychoanalytic and psychodynamic thinking. Healy's work with juvenile offenders was influenced by the psychosexual theories of Freud. Many of the youths he investigated had backgrounds sufficiently deviant to explain the etiology of their maladaptive behavior (Healy, 1934). Anna Freud (1928) advocated cooperative work with parents and teachers and advanced the adaptive and educational value of play therapy. The value of using social workers in the assessment procedures was recognized by these early pioneers in child treatment, and the model of teamwork among several disciplines eventually became standard procedure in child guidance clinics. A second thrust based on conventional wisdom that education begins at home fostered investigations into parent education and pedigoghy as the Child Study Association of America and the Parent/Teacher Association flourish. These groups have been responsible for an avalanche of child development guides to cover multiple facets of parenting and promoting the betterment of child as student. The impersonal, educational-oriented approach provides information to parents but is basically preventive in nature. While information and knowledge regarding the vicissitudes of children may thus deter the development of symptoms or maladaptive behavior, when such behavior occurs, a more person-oriented intervention of parents and children strive to foster better and more sensitive handling of difficulties, whether minor flare-ups within the parent/child relationship, or lowering of academic achievement, destruction of personal property or severe thought disorder.

The decades following World War II showed more and more children having dysfunctional reactions, having greater difficulties learning in school, and relating to authority figures. During the 1940s and 1950s, the collateral treatment of troubled children and their parents was the prevalent mode of intervention. These golden years of child guidance clinics saw an outpouring of factual knowledge about children and the widespread application of team methods for assisting parents and children (Halpern and Kissel, 1976). However, unfulfilled promises (Eysenck, 1965; Levitt, 1971; Leventhal and Weinberger, 1975; Kissel, 1974), the changing sociopolitical milieu that favored an autocratic-oriented technocratic leadership (Halpern and Kissel, 1976), and advances in medical management of emotional illness (Hollister, 1974) led clinicians to search for intervention strategies not routed in psychodynamic formulations of the mind. Practical, efficient and behaviorally oriented intervention strategies emerged as an answer to the dissatisfaction of clinicians with the dynamic psychoanalytic model as well as its variations which were the mainstream of child guidance clinics and the model which guided collateral intervention with parent and child. Behavior modification and family therapy emerged as powerful replacements for play therapy.

A confluence of a number of distinct events led to the emergence of behavior therapy. Wolpe (1956) and Wolpe and Lazarus (1966) applied the learning theory model of Hull to treat neurotic anxiety and phobic reactions with a process called reciprocal inhibition, or desensitization. B. F. Skinner (1954) "rediscovered" teaching machines and introduced instrumental or operant conditioning which became the basis for such varied treatment techniques as behavioral contracting, token management, consequent-oriented discipline and procedures for the management of hospital wards for psychotic patients.

Another major contribution to the therapeutic adaptation of learning principals can be attributed to the work of Bandura (1969) which emphasized modeling as an important ingredient in the learning and elimination of maladaptive behavior. A final and more recent trend has been the inclusion of cognitive components in behavior therapies (Goldfried and Davison, 1976; Mahoney, 1974; Meichenbaum, 1974).

Like its psychoanalytic forebearers, behavior modification techniques were initially applied to the treatment of adult psychopathology. As these approaches became more accepted in the mental health mainstream, they became modified so as to be applicable to children (Graziano, 1978; Halpern and Kissel, 1976; Kissel, 1972; Reisman, 1973).

Interest in play therapy was dwarfed by the family therapy movement which took hold during the mid-1960s and into the present. Changes away from the traditional directed and extended family, to a more egalitarian functioning body and a shift in functions from family to societal institutions set the stage for the emergence of family therapy. A sense of alienation and isolation between family members, disorganization, imbalance and strife propelled practitioners whose major expertness was in working with the family as an interacting unit (Kissel, 1980). Recently, there has been a reawakened interest by child psychotherapists in play therapy. As more and more children have been showing dysfunctional reactions and are having greater difficulties learning in school, and living in fractured, blended, or single-headed families with limited abilities to verbalize and relate to adults in authority, therapists have returned to working with children in the playroom.

The current renaissance in play therapy can be attributed to the following sociocultural developments: (1) high divorce rates, (2) blended families, (3) socioeconomic pressures requiring both parents to work, and (4) greater pressures for children to show academic proficiencies at younger ages. These events have been consistently shown to place children "at risk" for the development of emotional difficulties and adjustment problems. In addition, there has been a need in the professional community for increased understanding of treating children therapeutically.

For example, family therapists are, for the most part, talk-oriented, or those who have been trained to work with adults, at times, become puzzled and stymied what to do with children who after a session or two become "bored." The knowledge based on the principles of learning theory which resulted in behavior modification techniques were more readily applicable to adults and provided hope to parents that they might gain more power and more control in the relationship with their maladaptive child. Unfortunately, the promise has not been fulfilled.

Most of the earlier works on the theory and practice of child psychotherapy and play therapy were theoretical in orientation and directed intervention from a singular point of view. However, the modern-day child therapist tends to be more eclectic in orientation. A recent survey in the Rochester area in child intervention techniques brought out the serendipitous finding that clinicians were unable to be typed according to traditional theoretical affiliation.

Modern-day child psychotherapists borrow from many points of view as they attempt to map out ways of helping troubled and troublesome children. This is not surprising in light of the multitude of theoretical orientations which have emerged form the earlier writings of Sigmund Freud when he attempted to understand the workings of the mind and prescribe a treatment for mental disorders. Following on the heels of the orthodox child psychoanalysts who modified their work to fit the needs of their young patients came the non-directive therapist with their approach to children which was brought to its highest level of popularity by the work of Virginia Axline (1947) and Ginott (1965). Behavior modifiers, cognitive-oriented clinicians, and transactional analysts have had their time in the spotlight as well as puppeteers, art, music and movement therapists. Each in their own way has an effect on a generation of child therapists so that as we close the twentieth century, child clinicians have an array of intervention strategies for understanding their young patients and for successful intervention. While a theoretical orientation is significant in understanding and treating children, operating from a narrow point of view will limit clinicians in their range of understanding and intervention. When a child's maladaptive problems are understood from a singular point of view, then the clinician, more often than not, will attempt to fit the child to a point of view or force a particular intervention. However, with a broad-based eclectic orientation, a clinician will be able to tailor methods and strategies to fit the child rather than forcing each child to fit a particular mold. As early as 1965, I had been advocating such a position as has had Shaefer and his colleagues (Shaefer and Millman, 1977; Schaefer and O'Conner, 1983; Schaefer and Reid, 1986; Schaefer, 1988). In light of the changing social forces and the community mental health center movement throughout the 1960s, 1970s and 1980s, which placed much emphasis on providing broad-based comprehensive outpatient services to a diverse patient population, child clinicians must be prepared to be flexible in their approach to understanding and treating their young patients. They must be capable of deciding which strategy or technique will have greater likelihood for successful intervention. As we get ready to enter a new century, play therapists must be eclectic in nature rather than loyal to a single point of view which would limit their range of understanding and interventions. I will provide an approach to play therapy which will be broad in nature and allow child clinicians to borrow flexibly from already established theoretical positions and existing techniques. An orientation, however, which is atheoretical and provides only "recipes" as eclectic approaches of the past, will do little to help clinicians as they flounder among a myriad of techniques and strategies. For successful implementation of play therapy to occur, a theoretical orientation to provide clinicians with significant understanding in treating and choosing appropriate techniques is needed. It is this which sets the strategic approach to play therapy apart from some early, eclectic approaches to play therapy. Each clinician enters the playroom with an implicit or explicit conceptualization regarding children, a set of constructs to help in the understanding of children who behave in a maladaptive way, and a set of principals to guide interventions. Thus, it is important for the therapist to be clear as to their notions regarding children and their function as play therapists in the playroom. I will provide as clearly as possible an explanation of the activities and decision-making processes of the play therapist confronted by a variety of clinical exigencies. Play therapy from a strategic point of view consists of three major facets which encompass theoretical notions, therapists' concepts and an awareness of the tempo of the therapeutic process. The next section will provide the theoretical underpinnings for strategic play therapy. Background material pertinent to childhood developmental issues as they specifically relate to play therapy which clinicians need to be aware of when entering the playroom will be provided, as well as the multidimensional aspects of play. Differences between play and play therapy are also important distinctions which those doing play therapy have to be clearly aware of as well as having an understanding of why treatment which consists solely of talk is often inappropriate for children. Answers to these issues will also be considered. A non-traditional schema for assessing children's personality style and individual treatment plans (ITP's) are additional components of the strategic play therapist theoretic position.

Finally, principles which guide the clinician when entering the playroom, and what tools to bring to the playroom, will conclude the theoretical orientation to play therapy from a strategic point of view.

Following sections will ellaborate the second major element in the strategic play therapist approach: what the therapist does in the playroom. The strategic play therapist has three major functions: a modeling function, a mirroring function, and a maneuvering function. When modeling, the play therapist provides him or herself as a role model for the child and stresses the duality of protection and education; when mirroring, the therapist chooses from the myriad of verbal techniques which have proved valuable to therapists to convey to children their understanding, respect, and wish to be of help, and finally maneuvering which will describe the bag of tricks and techniques play therapists have at their disposal and often avoid using because of their uncertainty.

The final element of the approach revolves around the tempo of play therapy. In this section, guidelines for the initial encounter with children will be discussed and tactics for helping children with the difficult transition from playing for security and fun to living in the world outside of the playroom will be elaborated.

The psychotherapist who approaches play therapy from a strategic point of view is directive, active, and educationally oriented. We will focus our efforts only on the child and the work with the child in the playroom. This should not be construed as minimizing the importance of collateral contacts with parents or other child caretakers such as teachers, school administrators, baby-sitters and day-care centers. Such contacts are recognized by the strategic play therapists as an important part of the therapeutic package. Detailed discussions of collateral contact can be found in Halpern and Kissel (1976) and Reisman (1966).

CONCLUSION

The three major components to strategic play therapy are:

1. A theory section which elucidates a developmental understanding of children, the multifaceted functions of play and their relationship to therapeutic interventions and also a diagnostic schema which provides direction towards appropriate intervention strategies.
2. Therapist—This elucidates the triadic functions of the play therapist in terms of being a role model, mirroring the child's thoughts, feelings, and actions, and maneuvering by choosing appropriate intervention tools.
3. Tempo, which provides the play therapist with guidelines for directing the initial encounter with the child as well as knowledge regarding tactics for terminating the treatment as the child begins to move from the safety of the playroom to the trials and tribulations of living in the world beyond.

Chapter 2

BEFORE ENTERING THE PLAYROOM: THEORETICAL FOUNDATIONS

Before entering the playroom, therapists should have a conception, whether implicit or explicit, regarding children, what should occur during the time they spend with the child in play therapy, and how they will bring about change. In this chapter, I will highlight some key features of mental and personality development, drawing on the work of Jean Piaget and Erik Erikson. A child's mental and personality development is highly complex and is shaped by many interrelated forces. The present discussion makes no pretense of being comprehensive but will be selectively attentive to those elements which are of importance for clinicians as they understand a child's behavior in the playroom, formulate strategic interventions, or communicate their understanding to the child.

Clinicians, whether neophyte or seasoned facilitators, must keep in mind the distinction between play and play therapy. Furthermore, adult clinicians perceive treatment differently than children and the clinician must be aware of these distinctions. The adult must, so to speak, see the playroom and the time spent there with the child in therapy "through the child's eyes."

Clinicians unfamiliar with play therapy are often baffled by the array of toys in the playroom. A schema for choosing play equipment and organizing the play area to strategically foster therapeutic play will also be discussed. I will conclude the chapter with some general principles which can be viewed as analogous to a treasure map, guiding clinicians in their journey with their young patients to more adaptive behavior patterns and a realistic self-concept.

Some therapists believe there are minor differences between children and adults regarding psychotherapy in spite of their developmental differences. Others believe the cardinal difference is that adults and children harbor different feelings, while other therapists believe just the opposite. That is, while they believe children are able to experience feelings similar to adults, their thought processes are quite different from adults. It is this last view which guides the strategic play therapist. Different mental processes mediate one's ability to communicate and understand. Childhood is basically a developmental time in a person's life. Children need to mature—that is, internal processes have to unfold and these processes need nourishment from environmental stimulation—and parents and other significant caretakers have to encourage their physical, mental, and emotional growth.

Erik Erikson and Jean Piaget are two clinicians whose work has had a major impact on play therapists' understanding of a child's cognitive, emotional, and social development. For the most part, play therapy takes place with children between the ages of six to twelve. However, at times, late preschoolers, four- to five-year-olds, are seen in play therapy and benefit from treatment.

Children between the ages of birth and two develop what Erikson has labelled "a sense of trust" when all goes well. When parents are able to meet the preponderance of the infant's needs for nurturance, food and security, the child develops a stronger sense of trust than of mistrust. As the child's language and locomotive skills develop during these two years, the child is able to begin to explore his or her environment. The more the child feels that the parent will be available, the more successful their exploration will be. During the next two years, from ages two to four, children become more autonomous in their exploration of their external world and also begin to conquer their own body. When parents reward a child's successful actions and avoid shaming him or her for failures, then the child is more prone to take risks. For example, when attempting to gain bowel and bladder control, if encouraged and supported while having accidents, then the child's sense of autonomy will outweigh the sense of shame and doubt. This propels the child into the late preschool years from four to six where the major aspect of initiative is further developed. The child becomes quite curious and exploratory during this period, and if the child's need to know and to question is not discouraged but encouraged, the child's sense of initiative will outweigh the child's sense of guilt. It is during this time period that children are completing Piaget's second stage of development, which he called "the preoperational stage."

It is important for those who contemplate doing child treatment to be aware that during this period, children pay close attention to their own physical growth and appearance. Gender identity is formed with ensuing positive and negative attitudes toward one's sexuality. As children feel positive about their sexuality and their ability to master their body and pass in the external world, they begin to feel good about themselves, act independently, and develop more self-confidence. These traits are important as children become more and more involved with other children in nursery school and kindergarten programs. Parental love is of particular importance for children during this stage in helping them form positive self-images about themselves and function well in achievement-related situations.

Almost 50 years ago, Eric Fromm (1956) suggested a distinction between the type of loving ideally offered by mothers and fathers to their children. Motherly love is unconditional, whereas fatherly love is conditional. A mother's love cannot be earned or lost, because it is based not on what a child achieves or accomplishes but on a child's being. A mother's love relates to giving and can teach a child about doing for others, being affectionate, and giving as an expression of love.

A father's love depends upon what a child does and it can be earned or lost. Fatherly love teaches the child how to accomplish ends, deal with the world of things, and has as its legacy, courage, discipline, and self-control.

While Fromm's description of maternal and paternal love is idealized and perhaps oversimplified types, they do identify some key needs which have to be satisfied if the child is to make the most of his or her schooling, not feel burdened by shame, guilt, or inadequacy when initially failing at a task or making a mistake, and also to have sufficient internal guidesigns to make wise choices, avoid antisocial actions and have the discipline to strive for self-chosen goals. Both types of love are necessary and they provide the foundation of identity formation, and self-esteem.

Sharing is another aspect of childhood development whose foundations are laid during this stage. First born children have to learn to share parents' affection, either with a new baby, with older brothers and sisters, or with the parents, themselves. The younger sibling seems to get more attention, while the older sibling seems to have more privileges. It is aramount for parents to help the preschooler sustain their self-esteem and sense of competency in the face of these sibling rivalries by safeguarding their rights and reassuring them of their personal worth. Disturbed, multi-problem families, or families where one parent has to do double and triple duties, make it extremely difficult for the parent to provide such reassurance to the child. Socialization, especially early socialization, takes place in this preschool period during which time children acquire identification, respect for authority, self-discipline, and social judgment so necessary not only for growing into responsible adults but also for mastering the learning situation which will come soon.

Problematic families make it difficult for a child to achieve these early precursors of socialization. Discipline works best when it is administered consistently and when it has a teaching rather than a punitive aim. The main thrust of positive discipline is to help the child internalize the parents' rules and society's regulations so they can develop an internal sense of right and wrong and can behave according to these dictates away from the watchful eye of their parents. The self-confident child is more able to take chances, especially in new and unchartered situations, for, even if they fail, there is still an abundance of personal esteem to cushion their fall. A kindergarten teacher once characterized it this way to me:

> Imagine that each child's self-concept is a stack of poker chips. Some start school with a lot of chips, while others with very few. Now a student with 50 chips can sustain ten losses of five chips, while the child with ten chips can only sustain two losses of five chips each. The former student will be bolder while the latter will be considerably more cautious and reluctant to risk in new learning situations.

School ushers in the need for learning about the external world, developing more complimentarism regarding peer relationships and the striving for competency. The latency period of development which encompasses the middle years of childhood finds the child struggling with morality and moving towards greater investment of his energy in reality and the development of friendships. For most latency-age children, especially in the early phase, there is a greater acceptance of the demands and expectations of external authority figures. Improvements in gross and especially fine motor coordination are in evidence. As peer relationships become more important, childhood play changes from self-play to group play and then to group activities. Stronger attachments begin to be formed with people outside the immediate family as hostile and aggressive impulses and their derivatives are expressed in relationships with peers and significant adult figures.

The child's earlier curiosity and thirst for knowledge is now in full bloom. Children can develop strong feelings of inferiority at this time, if in addition to doing poorly in school they may be physically unattractive, awkward, unathletic, and berated frequently by parents. During the latency period, children are also most vulnerable to family disruptions due to parental separations or divorce.

Cognitive development effects and is effected by emotional and social development. The play therapist needs to be aware of the cognitive changes children undergo to be able to appropriately verbalize to the child and also know what the child may or may not be comprehending.

Piaget has described mental development as occurring in four stages. The sensory-motor is the first stage. We will not spend much time on this stage, as it has little relevance to play therapy with children. Each time children advance to another stage of development, they develop a higher level of thinking. The main thrust of the sensory-motor stage is the child's conquest of objects. Memory emerges as does rudimentary internalized thought as children are able to distinguish between present and absent, so that objects which are out of sight are not out of mind. The ability to symbolize brings the sensory-motor stage to an end and ushers in the second stage of Piaget's developmental theory which is called the preoperational stage. This stage usually occurs from age two to six. During the preoperational stage, the child has difficulty distinguishing between words and their reference (Elkind, 1970). For example, a child believes that an object cannot have more than one name and that a name inheres in the thing. During this stage, children's talk and verbalizations are quite idiosyncratic, and they believe that words carry more information than in fact they do. Children's language at this stage is reflective of their egocentrism and mirrors the limited perspective of their thinking. A child's language is filled with much repetition of what has already been stated by others and monologue directed to no one although stated in the presence of others. Several preschoolers together may engage in collective monologues where no real attempts at communication is made. Other manifestations in speech are: faulty use of pronouns, incorrect ordering of events, poor expression of causality, and omission of important features. During the early phase of this stage, children think anthropomorphically. They often believe that inanimate objects have characteristics similar to people and are alive. Furthermore, preschoolers perceive themselves as the origin of all activity and thus believe that an external event may be the direct result of their wishes or statements. Important family events such as sibling births and deaths, divorce, separations, and abuse can take on even greater proportions due to the child's magical thinking at this time of life. Children think that all objects are made for a purpose. Children's questions such as "Why do cats run on four legs?" "Why does the moon shine at night?" or "Why is grass green?" reflect their belief in the purposefulness of things. Elkind suggests a general rule for answering such "why" questions of children: "Begin the reply with a 'to' rather than with a 'because'." In "Little Red Riding Hood," the wolf, disguised as grandmother, replies to Little Red Riding Hood's, "My what big ears you have!" with "Better to hear you with...." The child's questions about nature can be answered in a manner which suits the child's intent and is factually correct. One can say with intellectual integrity that leaves fall "to cover the grass and flowers during the winter," and that the giraffe has a long neck to reach fruit that grows high in the trees" (1970, p. 31).

The child who is preoperational is able to use symbols and also has the ability to classify. Their advances in language development makes possible talking with children. They are also able to sort objects by shapes, colors, and sizes as well as showing spontaneous and also imaginative play. At this time, children are also able to take objects and use them to represent other objects. These developments make it possible to engage the preschool child in play therapy.

I was engaged in puppet play with an active, enthusiastic four-year-old. The play began to heat up, and rather spontaneously, he flicked the puppet at me and said, "You're dead, I shot you." It was very clear to me that the child had transformed the animal hand puppet into a gun. Play, more often than not, especially early in this stage, is more solitary than it is social. Such youngsters will feel quite content playing by themselves while they are being observed. It is also rather easy to have them play out both roles so that they will respond positively to such therapeutic comments as, "Why don't you do this while I watch." During the preoperational stage, a child's perceptions are quite centered. That is, they are unable to perceive or focus more than one dimension of a task at a time. Present a child two cups of water equal in volume and they will agree that both have the same amount of water. However, if one empties one of these into a different-shaped container, shorter and wider, the child will report that one or the other is larger. He has focused his thinking on one aspect of the cup's dimension, length or width, and ignored the reciprocal relationship between those dimensions. Similarly, their thinking does not include reverse ability, or the appreciation of the successive changes or transformations that take place in the water as it changes containers.

Children's thinking is sequential and not simultaneous, so they focus on one incident or object at a time. When a child's parents divorce, it is difficult for them to love both parents simultaneously and usually "love one, then they love the other." It is only with the introduction of the ability to conserve which occurs at the third stage of mental development—the concrete operational stage—that children can truly reason. At this time, children are more likely to be helped with such concerns as ambivalence, differences between their actions and their feelings, the ability to feel positive and negative towards a parent and/or feel positive towards two different parent-like adults, i.e. biological and stepmother, biological and foster parent. With the ability to conserve, the development begins to move from a more egocentric to a more sociocentric point of view. The child is able to think more objectively and loses considerably more of the anthropomorphic thinking of the preschooler. They are also able to look at situations with reciprocity, meaning they can take another person's point of view. Children also begin to show rudimentary relativistic thinking, although this does not come into full bloom until adolescence. The child is unable, until late latency and early adolescence, to distinguish between the public world of objects and the private world of thoughts and feelings. The preoperational child often believes that the parent is able to know what they feel and think and it is only into middle latency that children are aware that their thoughts and feelings are separate from their actions, and thus notions of confidentiality begin to make more sense. It is around ages six to eight years old that the concrete operational stage begins. The child can hold two distinct events, properties, or relations at the same time. For example: Two sticks of equal length are presented to a child in parallel position with the ends in alignment. After ascertaining that the child perceives them as equal in length, one stick is moved and while the preoperational child believes that one is now longer than the other, the child who is in the stage of concrete operations, being able to pay attention to the transformation, realizes that nothing has been added or subtracted and may say, "That's silly!" The symbol and the referent can be looked at simultaneously, but at this time, children have difficulty making a distinction between what it is they think and what it is they perceive. Youngsters will bend their perceptions in the external world to be congruent with their thoughts. They also believe that adults are not able to think as clearly as children and at times they will "secretly deviate" from many moral rules because they believe these rules come from adults whose authority they respect or fear but whose intellect they do not. Children are very much taken with mystery stories during this period because they like new, unexpected events which repeatedly occur and are mastered by the child. In some respects this accounts for the fascination latency-age children have with horror movies, which they like to watch over and over again. The latency-age child may have difficulties embracing this very important period of their development. They may show demandingness and dissatisfaction with what is given to them because of problems with the development of basic trust, or they may show stubbornness, withholding, and provocative behavior because of conflicts with their autonomous strivings, or they may even be overly compliant or suggestible because they are worried about losing the love of others. For such children, the play may be quite repetitive, i.e. building houses, towers, or playing house where they assume the role of the more powerful adult; or continually place the therapist in the role of a child. These are often tips that problems have befallen the child before entering latency and that they are unable to invest to their fullest effort and energy in mastering the social and emotional task of latency. They are unable to exercise their minds and follow rules, regulations, or enter into reciprocal relationships. These developmental tasks require the child to look beyond themselves to the external world and deal with problems of competition, cooperation, and comradeship. Such children appear not ready to learn about the culture of childhood, namely, learning patterns presented by the next older age group without attempts at radically changing them. Latency-age children, unlike adolescents, are not yet aware of the many constraints on success and by and large believe that they can become what they want to be. That is what they think! For most children, latency is a happy time because they are as of yet unable to fully conceptualize and understand the many problems and dangers of the external world, such as pollution or nuclear war, as their troubled adolescent brethren. While some of this is changing with the bombardment of newspapers and television, children still believe that the future will be what they wish it to be and therein lies the basis of their eternal optimism. Remember, if they can think about it, then it is so!

PLAY THERAPY

Psychotherapy evolved from psychoanalysis which was based upon the ability to free associate. The pre-latency-age child is not able to comply with free association, because the two- to six-year-old is action oriented and not word oriented. These children think according to primary rather than secondary process—that is, their thinking is inundated by their needs and wishes. Furthermore, children prior to latency and into early latency are less likely to obey the cardinal rule of talk therapy, which is say whatever comes into your mind. They are also not able to tolerate short-term anxiety for long-term gain. Children, whether problematic or not, have low frustration tolerance and especially children who have problems are unable to tolerate frustration, act out and are also unable to tolerate anxiety.

The latency-age child also has difficulty with the process of free association. More so than their younger colleagues, or adults, the idea that "talking will help" is a difficult concept for them to grasp. Talking to solve problems and express feelings, conflicts and attitudes requires language and thinking which is more sophisticated and subtle than available to the latency-age child. They have stronger resistance to looking at their inner impulse life. Latency is a time when children turn away from the inner world of impulses and move into the external world. There is a strong push to forget the past and indeed look to the present and future. The latency-age child has little motivation to "engage in the therapeutic contract" with the therapist. Often, they are in therapy because other people want them to be there, and, more often than not, they do not feel troubled but are "troubling." The responsibility for actions which cause conflicts for the latency-age child tends to be externalized. Finally, children are highly suspicious of the therapist, as the help to be offered usually follows a series of failed measures. It is not surprising that the child expects more reprimands, punishments, controls, and affronts to their self-esteem.

Play, a natural medium for children, is talk for a child in the playroom. Play serves many purposes for children. It gives them an opportunity to master actively that which may have been experienced passively. Play can also be thought of as preparation for the future and serve as a bridge between conscious thought and feelings and unconscious experiences.

During a play therapy session, a child is afforded the opportunity to express angry feelings and to find relief for past disappointments. Children's play begins with their own body and then moves towards playing with objects and people. Toys, especially manageable toys, can help the child master feelings they may have had about their body which caused earlier problems.

Play can be used by the play therapist for many purposes: It is used to help a child to release pent-up feelings such as sadness or anger. For example, the child can be helped to express anger in an appropriate, yet direct fashion. Substitutes such as punching bags, or pillows, or even fantasy constructions are provided as alternatives to inappropriate aggression. Play, with the tense and anxious child, can be used to mildly distract from worries so they can develop better coping strategies and skills. Board games, when used in treatment, provide children with many helpful insights into social and peer relations. Play is also use to help children overcome fears by encouraging them to actively master events indirectly or symbolically which they have experienced previously in a passive way. However, it is to be underscored that the friendly encouraging relationship which is formed between the child and the play therapist while engaged in play activities provides the backdrop and developmental nutrients for the child (attention, acceptance, and understanding) and is the cornerstone of correcting emotional dysfunctioning in children.

Strategic Assessment for Interaction

Each clinician enters the playroom not only with a conception of children but also with a particular categorization around which the child's behaviors, attitudes, feelings, and thoughts can be organized. For example, Harrington (1984) suggests understanding children from the DSM–III point of view and categorized childhood disorders into five broad areas: intellectual, behavioral, emotional, physical, and developmental. Quay (1972) considers childhood psychopathology from a behavioral point of view and suggests that four patterns account for a considerable amount of the aggression, withdrawal, and immaturity often found in children showing emotional disorders. The four dimensions are: immaturity, socialized delinquency, personality disorder, and conduct disorder. Anna Freud (1965) has provided a different and highly complex psychoanalytic conception of childhood pathology which is organized around the developmental task children experience.

The aforementioned approaches assist clinicians considerably as they attempt to understand the motivations for a child's maladaptive behavior and also when they consider the level of pathology of their young patients. However, these approaches have not been as enlightening or helpful in suggesting specific intervention techniques.

Throughout my years of supervising, teaching students and providing workshops and seminars, I have utilized a straightforward categorization which has been helpful in guiding clinicians to consider specific techniques for engaging children therapeutically, whether for a diagnostic assessment with the aim of gaining information or for a more sustained therapeutic interaction with the purpose of ameliorating maladaptive behaviors and traits. For this purpose, children who are having problems can be thought of as either being *too loose* or *too tight.*

Too tight children are fearful, anxious, and have considerable difficulty expressing themselves verbally or behaviorally because they often are afraid of letting go. Children who are too loose, on the other hand, have a considerable amount of difficulty controlling their impulsive and behavioral expression of thoughts or feelings. They seem to lack concern regarding the feelings of others, have difficulty anticipating the effects or consequences of their behaviors, and have been reinforced in the past for excessive nonverbal expressions. Their ability to control themselves is poorly developed. Of course, both types of problem youngsters have difficulty with their self-esteem, as a history of maladaptive behavior often leaves significant others in the environment to accentuate the negative and eliminate the positive when interacting with these children. Both types of youngsters often find it difficult to verbalize their thoughts and feelings directly. Those who are too loose cannot stand still long enough to reflect upon their performance, or they compare themselves with others negatively. In general, children manifesting anxiety or depressive disorders are found to be too tight, whereas conduct and attention deficit children are found to be too loose. Whether a child is conceived of as being too loose or too tight depends on more than his or her overt behavior. For example, preschoolers and latency-age children who are stressed may manifest their upset through disturbance in bodily functions. Soiling, bed-wetting, sleep disturbance, or motor abnormalities are surface behaviors which may suggest that a child is out of control and too loose while in fact the child is basically too tight. The purpose of seeing a child as too loose or too tight is not suggested as an alternative to more traditional categorization or diagnostic formulations but rather as a device for considering some effective and efficient techniques for engaging the child. This schema can be used to augment traditional treatment plans so that the therapist can be more specific in how he will go about maneuvering with the child to ameliorate a symptom which may be too loose or too tight. Very succinctly, tight children need to be loosened and loose children need to be tightened.

The table below provides a list of materials commonly found in the playroom arranged according to the too loose-too tight schema.

Loosening	Tightening Up
clay/play dough	construction: sewing
crayons	models
paints	glue
paper	cards
finger paints	board games: Sorry
blocks	checkers
darts, dart board	any game with rules
punching bag	mirrors
water	video recorders
sand box	balls

Puppets, animals, and people as well as a dollhouse and its furnishings, doctor kits, play money, and a blackboard are other staples of the playroom which can be used for either purposes of loosening or tightening.

Five guiding principles which can be kept in the front, back, or middle of your head as you engage children in the playroom brings to a close the theoretical orientation to play therapy from a strategic point of view. The guiding principles are:

1. The relationship is the key to success.
    a. Develop a warm, friendly relationship.
    b. Be an authority, not an authoritarian.
    c. Be permissive regarding expression of feelings; set appropriate limits regarding expression of action.
2. Accept the child as he/she is:
    a. Help child distinguish between wishes, feelings, and actions.
    b. Recognize child's feelings and reflect them back to child to further understanding and insight.
    c. Whenever possible, relate child's thoughts and feelings to behavior.
3. Respect the child's ability to solve his/her own problem.
    a. Help child see choices.
    b. Encourage child to make decisions and take responsibility.
4. Establish limits that are necessary to anchor the therapy to reality and make the child aware of his/her contribution to the relationship.
5. Therapy works best when therapist recognizes that therapy is a process and should not be hurried to satisfy external pressures.

Chapter 3

ARRIVING AT THE DOOR: THE ROLE OF THE PLAY THERAPIST

The play therapist's behavior can be conceptualized as unfolding in recognizable patterns which vary along three major dimensions. It is these dimensions which will comprise the material of the next chapters:

A. The first dimension, a modeling dimension, consists of what the play therapist brings of himself or herself to the play therapy room.

B. The second dimension is the attitude the play therapist conveys to the child regarding his or her understanding of the child as a person, as well as his understanding of the child's problem. This dimension is characterized as mirroring.

C. The bag of tricks or maneuvers the therapist brings to the playroom as she interacts with the child and attempts to help him overcome his dilemmas and problems.

MODELING

First and foremost, child psychotherapists present themselves as role models to their young patients. In doing so, they convey to the child that they are a person of authority in the playroom. They let the child know this by their actions as well as by their words. The child therapist maintains control in the playroom by not permitting anything to occur which is harmful to either the child or to the therapist. It is the therapist's responsibility to see that the playroom is adequately stocked and, furthermore, that the tools and materials that are present are appropriate and not broken nor nonfunctional.

The task of stocking the playroom falls upon the therapist. As mentioned in the previous chapter, the toys which the play therapist uses can be analogous to tools which other healers have at their disposal as they attempt to work with their patients. The playroom should not be overly messy, as this may contribute to confuse the child or inappropriately stimulate the child. By the same token, the playroom cannot be a sterile operating room, either. From time to time, play therapists may engage in the construction of projects with their child. Such projects which are left from session to session need to be cared for so that other children do not inadvertently destroy or lose parts of uncompleted projects. Thus, the child therapist will show that he is an authority and in control by providing a safe and comfortable environment for the child. The safety will be demonstrated from the initial encounters which the child has with the play therapist. For example, a child may see a dart board in the room and show interest in playing but then express concern that the darts are not pointed like the one's he is used to playing with. The therapist can take this as an opportunity to verbalize the fact that in the playroom the darts have suction because they are less likely to hurt anyone or cause accidents or be destructive to the walls of the playroom.

Another youngster who waves a dart gun in the direction of the therapist may be greeted by such words as, "People are not for shooting at," or "If you are angry with me, you can shoot at a picture of me or at the punching clown." However, depending upon the therapist's internal feelings and movements, the verbalizations can be congruous or can provide the child with an incongruous message. If you back away from the child while redirecting verbally, you suggest to the child that you are fearful or worried and are not in control. Whereas if you move toward the child while talking with him or her about such limits, you convey to the child a greater sense of control.

Many children, especially those who act up and have poor frustration tolerance, are used to losing parts and being reprimanded for their messiness. They also tend to be punished by having things taken from them so that there is often a sense of deprivation. It is important that while working with such youngsters, they have their projects cared for and that they find intact what it is they are working on. This conveys to the child that the psychotherapist is consistent, caring, and can provide protection for their objects which can then be generalized so that the psychotherapist can provide protection against their inner impulses and that his or her protective stance can be internalized as an alternative to their other introjects. This is the beginning of a changed internalization or representation for object relationships: relating to other people.

How the therapist is viewed by the child also is evidenced in the manner in which they play. The areas of cooperation and competition are often played out. Before discussing the pitfalls which a therapist may become involved in with a child, especially when engaged in board games, the question of "To play or not to play" will be considered.

This is a question which has plagued therapists who work with children. One school of thought believes playing with children is positive because it will provide an alternative to a depriving or cruel parent and thus may neutralize some of the ill effects of earlier parental interactions while maintaining a closer contact and interrelationship with the child. Another school of therapy believes that play therapy is hindered when a play therapist participates in activities with the child and thus may be viewed as either a parent or a playmate. They see that playing with the child can undermine some of the unique interactive aspects which a therapist brings to the playroom.

I take a mid-position, in that at times it is helpful to be engaged and play with the child; at other times it is more helpful to maintain distance. The play therapist in his or her modeling capacity is not only a provider of safety but is also a teacher of interpersonal relations and a model who children often introject as they do other significant others as they mold their personality. Direct interactive play facilitates rather than hinders change, although it does cause more thoughtfulness on the part of the therapist as they have more decisions to ponder than if guided by the caveat, "Do not play with the child, but suggest that the child play for both of you while you watch."

When involved in board games where there is a competitive aspect, the therapist will focus on the child's feelings, attitudes and style more so than on winning or losing the game. Some beginning therapists believe it is important to permit children to win or their feelings will be hurt if they lose. This is a tactical error. Better to focus on the child's reaction to realistic loss and to their developmental limitations while stimulating hopefulness in the future. Board games also call out a need and wish on the part of the child to win, and often young children will cheat to accomplish their aims. This, too, causes dilemmas for the therapist. Many children who cheat often do so because their self-esteem is associated in their minds with winning or losing and they tend to believe that their therapist evaluates them on the basis of whether or not they win the game. When a child is observed cheating, the cheating can be likened to rules, which is important for latency-age children. The therapist needs to recognize with the child that it is important for him to win, label that the rule has been changed and suggest that it is appropriate to change the rules just as long as it happens before playing begins, but that once the rule is in force, both child and therapist have to abide by the rule.

At times, it is also helpful to make comments to the child about your views regarding evaluations of children and their self-esteem. You may suggest to children that you do not evaluate them or think of them on the basis of whether they win or lose the game, but that their are many other more important characteristics of children that are used to determine what kind of a person they are. In essence, the therapist reflects the child's wish and need to win while also mentioning the awareness that the rule has been changed. Likening cheating to rule violation changes for both child and therapist an experience which is often fraught with conflict and also provides alternatives for the child to handle similar situations as they occur with peers without necessarily talking about the particulars.

A second major area where the therapist shows that he is an authority and in control of what occurs in the playroom has to do with the setting of limits and the handling of aggression.

Limits which are set in play therapy must be fair and enforceable. It is important, however, that they not be set in advance but rather as behaviors emerge from the interaction between the child and the therapists. Ginott (1959) has suggested a four-step procedure for limit setting which has been implicitly or explicitly adapted by most child therapists. He suggests:

1. Limits direct catharsis into symbolic channels.
2. Limits enable the therapist to maintain attitudes of acceptance, empathy, and regard for the child client throughout the therapy contact.
3. Limits assure the physical safety of the children and the therapist in the playroom.
4. Limits strengthen ego controls.
5. Some limits are set for reasons of law, ethics, and social acceptability.
6. Some limits are set because of budgetary considerations. It is clear from these principles that the therapist not only provides for the safety of the child but is teaching what is acceptable behavior and also redirecting a child's unacceptable expressions into more acceptable channels.

Limits can be set using the following four steps:

1. Recognize the child's wish and help the child express this wish. For

example, "I understand that you would like to take that toy home with you."
2. State the limit: "Toys are for playing in the playroom."
3. Suggest alternatives: "It will be here for us to play with next week." "You may have something similar like that you can play with at home." "If you want, you can think about the toy so that we will play with it."
4. Reflect feelings and help the child express some resentment: "I understand that you are angry, that you are not able to take the toy home."

In essence, the approach labels clearly what the child would like to do, states the limit and recognizes that the child has some feelings about the limit, and, wherever possible, provides some substitute outlet for the expression of these feelings.

Confidentiality

Another area where the therapist has opportunities to demonstrate that he is a caring and trustworthy person has to do with the realm of confidentiality. Counselors, caseworkers, and psychotherapists are often more comfortable with their handling of confidentiality as it applies to their adult patients. The handling of confidentiality with children, however, is somewhat different than with adults. Many novice play therapists often error on the side of disregarding the child's wishes and needs and thus attempt to get the parent on their side so they may divulge too much, while others error on the side of alienating and distressing parents with a rigid adherence to the view of confidentiality that, "I can't talk about that with you because it is confidential." Children are dependent upon adults, whether it be their parents or some other legal adult who is responsible for them. Thus, it is not sound practice, nor, for that matter, ethical or legal, to work with a child without obtaining the permission of his or her parent. Furthermore, it is the parent who brings and pays for the child in play therapy. A related issue has to do with what information the therapist will convey to the child regarding contacts they have had with a child's parent. Usually, a discussion of confidentiality will come up with the child somewhere during the first few sessions and usually before a meeting would occur with a child's parent. If the child shows some reluctance, strong resistance or is inhibited to play or talk with the therapist, it is especially important to talk some with the child about concerns they may have regarding whether or not what they say and do will be divulged to their parents.

The following guides may be helpful in handling the issue of confidentiality in a way which conveys to the child that his needs and wishes are of paramount importance to the therapist and that you as a therapist are a trustworthy person. The concept of absolute confidentiality which is often given to adults must be modified when considering children, whether seen privately or (as in the case of many children) at a social agency. The confidentiality cannot be absolute in child guidance work due to the fact that many other clinicians may be involved in the case and will have to talk with each other. Furthermore, usually the parent has had contacts with clinic staff prior to their child being seen for evaluation or therapy. Similarly, it is important for the parent to be aware that the confidentiality, while being limited, will be involved both ways. Thus, it is not in the best interest of movement in play therapy to tell children something such as, "Everything you do and say with me is between the two of us and I won't tell your parents about it." It is much better to let the child know that you will be meeting with their parents from time to time and that, while you will not share exactly what happens, you will share your impressions with their parents, or, if their parents are seeing another staff person at a clinic, that you will talk with that other person who is talking with the child's parents so that "We can all help the family to become better." For the most part it is not necessary to discuss the specific talk or symbolic play, although discussion of the child's play can help bring some insights into the family interaction without necessarily divulging confidences. Reisman (1973) has suggested a number of guidelines which have been helpful for therapists working with children.

1. The therapist should divulge nothing about the content of the contacts he has with the child without first securing permission from the parents. Even though the child may be your client, the parents have the authority to give or deny the therapist permission to communicate about his or her work with others such as positions or school personnel.
2. Before talking with anyone about his client such as parents or school personnel, the child should be informed of the meeting and asked regarding his or her wishes for anything in particular to be

divulged or whether there is anything the child wishes not communicated. At times it is helpful to invite the child to attend such meetings.

3. At times, confidentiality will have to be broken to protect the child from committing some aggressive or destructive behavior. When this occurs, the child should be informed that confidentiality will be breached and discuss with the child his wish or need for external controls.
4. Often, children will give the therapist permission to say "anything" in meetings they may have with parents or significant others. It is important for the therapist to be extremely careful what is divulged and as a general rule not provide information regarding the content of sessions with children. It is often helpful to direct parents to discuss their interests with the child, and should the parents respond that the child is reluctant to talk with them, then the therapist can encourage the parents to respect their child's wish. Under such circumstances, at times, it may be helpful to arrange a meeting between parents and child to discuss some of these issues.

One of the reasons, as discussed in Chapter 2, that play therapy is difficult is due to the fact that children are often mistrustful of adults, as they have been reprimanded and criticized for their problematic behavior and expect the same of the therapist. Furthermore, the child enters their involvements with play therapists with preconceived notions regarding what the therapist may be. Children test their views regarding the therapist just as therapists test their hypothesis regarding what may be disturbing to the child. Often, the child attempts to place the therapist in the role of a teacher or of a parent. For example, children may pick up objects which they clearly know and say, "What is this?" or they may say, "Is this a telephone?" The wise therapist will answer with a question, "What is it?" or "What do you think?" Not only is such innocuous chitchat between child and therapist likened to adults discussing the weather or boxers beginning to feel each other out, but it is also a way for the child to see whether or not the therapist will respond to him the way other adults might. Children may also wonder about how toys can be used or whether or not the therapist will catch him in simple calculational errors or instruct him how to spell words which he can already spell. A good rule of thumb is for the therapist to inform the child that in the playroom he could add or spell however he would like to. Questions regarding broken toys may also come up where the child is really attempting to find out what will happen if he or she accidentally breaks a toy. Some benign comment regarding the fact that mistakes sometimes happen will be reassuring and will suffice. The child is also trying to find out whether or not the therapist will get angry with him.

The child psychotherapist is a role model for the child and very clearly demonstrates her wish to be of help and his respect for the child by teaching him by both words and by deeds. He provides a safe haven for the child to begin to risk expressing himself and learning better ways of handling her impulses. The therapist conveys an accepting attitude while not condoning maladaptive behavior through the appropriate setting of limits and interacting with the child around play in a cooperative and ego-enhancing fashion. His manner is such that he stimulates hope in the future rather than despair or anxiety in the present. While providing him or herself as role models, therapists are also engaging in a multitude of verbal exchanges with the child and thus they are engaged in techniques of mirroring. This is the subject of our next chapter.

Chapter 4

TALKING WITH CHILDREN IN THE PLAYROOM: MIRRORING

In the last chapter, I discussed the role-modeling aspects of the play therapist, and in this chapter, I will focus on the mirroring aspects of play therapy. The therapist can use a number of verbal techniques to convey to the child that he or she understands their emotional needs, that he understands the child's problems, and most importantly that she wishes to be of help to the child with his or her problems in a respectful relationship.

There are a number of decisions the therapist has to make. The therapist needs to decide whether his verbal comments will focus on the emotional or the cognitive aspects of an exchange. The therapist will furthermore have to decide whether the verbalization will convey support, be more probing, or depth oriented and whether or not the exchange will provide the child with some closure, left open-ended, or stimulate some uncomfortable affect.

Along these aims, therapists have a number of verbal interactive techniques at their disposal.

Supportive Interventions

In the supportive role the therapist's comments provide a benign and permissive environment. In such a relationship some regressive needs such as dependency often are evoked and thus can be satisfied, thereby reducing the need for such gratification through symptoms. At such time, a free discussion of practical problems can stimulate children to use their intellectual capacity; catharsis can help to reduce tension and anxiety levels, leading the child to feel better about him or herself. The status of the therapist, vis-á-vis the child in the relationship, provides help to instill confidence in the child. *Attentive listening* is one major technique used by play therapists when mirroring in a supportive role.

Play therapists engage in attentive listening by attending to the verbal and nonverbal communication and commenting upon some reflectory tendency, pointing out a discrepancy between a child's intention (wishes and attitudes and their execution, behavior), or reflecting on their own puzzlement regarding a child's comments or actions. The focus in attentive listening is usually on an incongruity between what is said and how the communication is stated. For example, after listening to a mother describe the number of major battles between herself and her daughter, I said to the woman, "You keep insisting Sally take more responsibility; yet, when she suggests her own way of doing something, you seem to find fault."

Related is the technique of *unblocking*.

Labelling and verbalizing feelings that are softly spoken can also help convey to a child that you have understanding of his or her needs. For example, a child came into the playroom, sat down and looked around in silence. I reflected on the child's puzzlement and uncertainty about being in the playroom.

Another child verbalizes and talks in a pseudo-sophisticated fashion about his worries, yet his eyes dart at the pictures hanging in the playroom, at the easel, and at the toy chest. It is clear from his behavior that he is more interested in playing than talking, yet the child seemed to believe or may have been instructed that he or she is supposed "to talk to the doctor." I commented, "It seems you are curious about what is in the different drawers and you are certainly interested in the paintings on the wall. I wonder if you are thinking about whether you would like to paint or play?"

Yet, another reflective comment which therapists do when mirroring has been called *reflexive explorations*, which are statements in which the therapist rephrases what the child said. When done successfully, the rephrasing (a) adds some meaning to what the child said and (b) encourages the child to go on exploring his or her feelings. An example of reflexive exploration is the following interaction:

Child: Every day a different kid teases me at school.

Therapist: Yes, I can see by your expression that you have a lot of feelings about it.

Notice the therapist is adding his or her perception of the child's present state and leaves the comment open-ended in a way that encourages the child to continue. This is an extremely useful technique that can be used frequently. However, it can also be overused. Its goal is to explore and make children aware of their feelings.

Related to reflexive explorations is the pure restatement of what the child says. The purpose of a restatement is to encourage the child to continue to talk and/or elaborate some informational or cognitive aspects of a comment.

Uncovering Interventions

When play therapists mirror in an uncovering role, they use all of the aforementioned supportive techniques, environmental manipulation, defense strengthening, but, in addition, interpretation, insight, and working through. These techniques are often associated with dynamic psychotherapy or psychoanalysis.

Interpretation is the process whereby the therapist helps the child relate something which is occuring or upsetting in the present with past or seemingly non-related events.

Child: I am tired of not having friends. Each time I think I might be able to get to know somebody and make a friend, something seems to go wrong.

Therapist: Perhaps you have something to do with these breakups.

For an interpretation to be successful, the patient has to be aware of the present feelings and thoughts in question and the past experience that is being related.

Insight is the patient's true as distinct from a merely verbal understanding of the origins and unconscious dynamics of his or her behavior.

Working through is a re-exploration of a problem situation tracing its symbolic meaning to "deep" unconscious sources in order to find a satisfactory solution or adaptation to the problem.

Additional Helpful Verbalizations

Reisman (1976) has suggested a number of other helpful verbalizations.

1. Empathetic statements—statements a therapist makes to convey understanding of a child's feelings can be labeled empathetic statements:

Child: Whenever I have to present in class or when the teacher looks in my direction when he asks the class to answer a question, I feel all shaky. I don't know why I should feel this way. It is the silliest thing.

Therapist: This both upsets and puzzles you.

2. Interrogative statements. The therapist attempts to convey his wish to be of help and to understand the client's communication by requesting more information or clarification.

Client: When I found out I failed all my courses, I decided not to show my parents my report card.

Therapist: What did you think that would do?

3. Expository statements. The therapist presents his understanding, point of view, or analysis so that the child or family will gain a clearer understanding of the problem under discussion:

Child: Boy, what a mess I got myself into this time. Once again, I acted without thinking. I have to stop and think so that I can begin to act differently.

Therapist: Let's go over the situation and think about some things you might have done.

4. Responsive statements. The therapist acknowledges the child comments by conveying her attentiveness to the child's comment. The therapist thus encourages the client to continue with his narrative.

Child: Johnny makes me feel as if he is out for revenge.

Therapist: Hmmm.

5. Confrontation. This is a technique which should not be used often. It involves a battle of wills, suggesting an affect or attitude which is dimly perceived by the child—for example, children who comment that they are unhappy about coming for therapy, but continue to come, are engageable and seem to enjoy the therapy; children who behave in treatment as if they do not hear what you are saying, yet by their action and their facial expressions convey that they are aware, but do not want to acknowledge their awareness because to do so would require further involvement, verbalizations, or experienced feelings.

Confrontational messages from the therapist to the child regarding unacceptable behavior of the child, regarding broken rules of the playroom or regarding the therapist's reaction, if not done carefully but as a subtle expression of a therapist's anger, can be damaging to the child's self-esteem and diminish the therapeutic relations. Destructive confrontational interventions often occur when the child is resistive to becoming involved in the relationship and the therapist feels threatened. His/her confidence or esteem as a therapist is based on the ability to get the child involved, or to like him/her.

When a child frustrates the therapist's efforts to help the child to reveal aspects of him/herself in order to recognize problems, this can be perceived as the child depreciating the therapist's wish to be of help. A tip-off that the confrontational message may be a destructive one is what Gordon (1974) has called "You message," i.e. "*You* shouldn't do that." The following are examples of more appropriate confrontational messages: "We, I or rule messages."

A child throws something at the therapist.

Therapist: Ouch! That really hurt me! People are not for shooting at. . . .

A child ignores the therapist's comment.

Therapist: I know you can hear what I'm saying. Sometimes you like to pretend you can't hear me.

For the most part, depth-oriented and interpreted verbalizations are reserved for older children, while supportive verbalizations are usually used with the younger, latency-aged child. Interpretive statements made by the therapist to younger children are more effective when made within the context of play and reserved for puppets, animals or dolls.

A child therapist may make suggestions to children either directly or indirectly as an expression of their wish to help. When a child suggests through words or play that they are tense, anxious, worried (too tight), the child therapist may suggest some techniques for alleviating or lessening the tension and may read a child a story which will be ego bolstering or have specific suggestions embedded within the story. Similarly, aggressive controlling techniques may be offered as a way of forestalling acting-out behaviors.

When the child therapist uses suggestion, more often than not, it is in conjunction with some specific maneuver which will be the focus of the next chapter.

Praising Children

Some therapists do not believe in praising a child in the playroom because they fall into the "blank screen" trap: they want to be perceived as a neutral figure so that the child can project some distortions of personality and interpersonal relations. Yet, other therapists also refrain from providing praise because they perceive praising a child as compromising their non-evaluative stance: "Praise today, criticize tomorrow." However, if done judiciously and with care, praise can contribute to bolstering a child's self-esteem, encourage greater risk taking and/or provide positive rewards for controlled behavior. The real question is not whether a therapist should or should not praise a child during play therapy sessions but rather when and how.

It is important that the therapist praise a child only occasionally and not in an overenthusiastic fashion so that the child becomes more interested in pleasing the therapist rather than him or herself. When praising a child, keep these points in mind:

1. Place control in the child's hands. That is, tell the child how proud he or she must feel by remembering the rule instead of telling the child how proud you feel regarding the child's accomplishment.

2. Point out the child's progress and effort. "You sound really pleased with your test score. You spent a lot of time studying and it really paid off."

3. Be specific. Use concrete descriptors rather than evaluative words. When discussing a child's work, instead of telling a child how pretty, nice or beautiful a picture is, you can describe the different colors used as a means of encouragement.

The mirroring techniques are a series of verbal interactions which can help the child become aware of feelings and attitudes, express feelings and attitudes, explore options, and become more aware of the contributions he or she makes to a problem. The more children can be helped to formulate broad governing rules or concepts, the greater is the likelihood that they will generalize from the playroom to other situations. In addition to conveying your wish to be of help and understanding of the child's problems, your verbal comments can provide the ingredients for some lasting change by helping the child generalize some newfound attitudes and ideas in the playroom.

Chapter 5

PLAYING WITH CHILDREN IN THE PLAYROOM: MANEUVERING

Therapists maneuver for many different purposes. At times, they maneuver to help uptight children ventilate their feelings. This assists the child in discharging pent-up feelings as well as helping to clarify how the child feels, and towards whom the feelings are directed. Such tasks as punching an inflatable bag or throwing darts can be very helpful.

> For example, a seven-year-old's major presenting problem was that he would tic whenever he was called to talk in front of his classmates. He would often evidence the tic whenever we spoke about his father and as he began some sequence of puppet play with large animals or the father puppet. When the tic was manifested, it often diminished or disappeared as the play became more overtly aggressive. After a few sessions, I shared my observation with him and suggested that it seems to be helpful when he gets his "mad out," and suggested he use the punching bag.

Therapists maneuver to help children who are loose bind anxiety. This can be analogous to fidgety, anxious adults doodling while listening to a presentation or fingering worry beads when they are upset. The squeezing of slime or playing with clay or even drawing scribbles while talking about difficult material can sometimes be helpful. Related to the binding of anxiety is using such tools as board games or construction type tasks such as models or crafts. In addition to binding anxiety, construction tasks can focus the child to following rules and emphasize controlling techniques. The inability of some children to control themselves or follow rules are often the basis for triggering their anxiety. Essentially, they are concerned about losing control, behaving maladaptively or acting aggressively, which has led to a reprimand from an adult, parent or teacher. The loss of control for loose children is a strong stimulus to feeling inadequate due to their own inability to control themselves despite their externalizing of responsibility for their loss of control.

Yet another reason therapists maneuver with children is to loosen them up with the use of regressive play tools. Fingerpainting, sandbox play, and smearing encourage children to act and are often helpful.

Pseudomature, tense children are often worried about playing with the therapist for fear of either acting like a baby or getting dirty. Both concerns are repressed from conscious awareness, and often with some encouragement these children will throw themselves into such play.

Therapists will also use play as a means to understand children and their problems as well as for indirectly communicating to a child. Play, as previously discussed, is a child's symbolic talk and it can be used to work through a problem with a child or to communicate through the play solutions to problems, a wish to help and understanding. Storytelling type games where the major emphasis is on communication such as the Talking, Doing, and Feeling game, Social Security, or Conversation as well as storytelling, or the squiggle game will foster such symbolic communication.

> The parents of an eight-year-old reported her to be shy, cry easily and constantly complain about not having friends. During a therapy session with the youngster who was having difficulties relating to peers, we played the squiggle game and she told a brief story about a tree growing by itself on a hill.
> I asked her to make a squiggle for me and responded by drawing a couple of trees and yet another tree separate from the group. I created a story about the separate tree who felt sad and lonely and wished to play with the other trees but was afraid to speak with them. I had the wind blow the branches of the tree in their direction so that the other trees noticed and they began talking. I suggested that the meaning of my story was that it is helpful to speak to others.

Therapists will make specific suggestions to teach a child specific behaviors which may help reduce anxiety or further self-control. In this capacity, a therapist may teach a child muscle relaxation, breathing exercises or anger controlling techniques.

SPECIFIC TOOLS

DRAWING TECHNIQUES: THE DRAW-A-DOG GAME

Drawing is well suited especially for engaging uptight children. Younger uptight children are made especially uncomfortable by new situations, such as the first time they meet a new therapist. Extreme inhibition, silence, or an inability to enter into play activities are some common manifestations. This picture-drawing game (Fig. 1) provides a way of quickly reducing anxiety while enlisting the child's involvement in an activity which is pleasant, non-threatening, and consistent with both egopsychoanalytic formulations of anxiety and a Piagetian theory of mental development. While playing this game, especially during the early encounter, the practitioner is concrete and "giving" rather than overly verbal, reflective, or "depriving."

After introducing yourself to the child, ask "Have you ever played a picture-drawing game?" and immediately go to the easel and draw a square on a piece of paper. Then say, "Once upon a time there was a house," and proceed to draw in the square two smaller squares for windows and one rectangle for a door as shown in Figure 1, Drawing A. Continue by stating, "It was just like any other house with two windows, a door, a roof, and two chimneys." Add a triangle to the top and then two chimneys coming off either side as in Drawing B. "In the house there lived a little (boy/girl)." To this point you have asked nothing of the child but have given some perceptual stimulation by drawing a picture and having presented some words in a child-oriented tone. Now ask the child for a name. After a sufficient period of time if the child does not provide one, you provide the child's name and ask for his or her acknowledgment. (For purposes of our example, let the name be John.)

"Okay now, John lived in this house with his parents. One day John's parents brought him a pet doggie; what did John call his pet doggie?" As before, wait for the child to provide a name and if he or she does not, you do so. (For our example, let's call the dog Spot.) "Every day as John would go to bed he would take his pet dog Spot with him. One day when John got up, he didn't find Spot in his room. He walked out in front of the house and did not see Spot there." Upon that draw a straight line from the door of the house as in Drawing C. If the child responds no, agree with him; if he responds yes, say, "John went to the door, and when he got close he saw the dog looked like Spot but wasn't Spot." If the child makes no response after a reasonable time, state, "He didn't find Spot." The next part of the game consists of drawing a number of lines so that they look like feet as in Drawing D. While making these lines, say the following: "John began to look for his dog Spot; he went on one street and up another and then to another." You can pause and ask the child if he sees his dog; the response in all cases which you are looking to elicit is no. Should the child say yes, repeat as previously that he walked to the dog but it wasn't Spot. Get to the point where four legs are drawn and then tell the child, "John remembered that Spot liked to run in the park, so he ran there," and draw a line which will become the tail. Ask the child if he found Spot; there the answer again should be no. While asking him that question, draw a bushy tail and tell the child, "John kept looking and looking in the park for his dog but could not find him," as in Drawing E.

Next, ask the child how John felt; the appropriate response is "sad." Then ask the child whether John walked home fast or slowly; regardless of what the child says, state that he felt sad and walked home slowly as in Drawing F.

Upon drawing the final line from the tail back to the house, the child should be asked, "What happened to the picture of the house?" Some children will immediately say "Spot came home," others will say "It looks like a dog," and others will seem puzzled. In any case, let the child know that the house became a picture of a dog, and ask if he or she would like to take it home. Following this you can begin to talk with the child, suggest that he or she might want to play with some toys, or, as I often do, ask the child to make a picture for me, either of a person, his or her family, an animal, or whatever.

Basically, the child has been given something to take home and has been engaged in a hierarchical fashion, as you first give and then demand a little, and then demand somewhat more during the interview. Finally, the child has been asked to produce something in return which can provide diagnostic information, and also has been related to in a less threatening, anxiety-reducing fashion.

The preceding picture story game can be followed by a number of other drawing tasks. If the therapist is more interested in obtaining diagnostic information, the more helpful standardized techniques, such as the Draw-A-Person or Kinetic Family Drawing, other drawing tasks such as Squiggle (Winnicott, 1951; Claman, 1980), Draw-A-Fear (Crowley and Mills, 1987; Kissel, 1984) or variants of Art Therapy (Horovitz, 1983; Kramer, 1977), are more therapeutic.

Figure 1. The Picture Drawing Game

Draw-A-Person

The Draw-A-Person (DAP) has found wide acceptance by mental health workers as they attempt to comprehend the mental abilities and personality styles of troubled and troublesome children (Sundberg, 1961). Since Goodenough introduced a standardized approach for using drawings to assess intelligence in 1926, the Goodenough DAP test has been successfully used in a multitude of settings such as schools, hospitals, clinics, community mental health centers, and counseling centers with a wide variety of populations. Indeed, surveys have demonstrated that the DAP is among the five most frequently used assessment procedures (Lubin, Wallis, and Paine, 1971; Sundberg, 1961).

Since the introduction of the DAP test, many variations of the test have been introduced. A number of major reviews have been written regarding the reliability and validity of the test as a measure of intelligence, and the signs of personality disruption that can be generated from interpreting the drawing. Reviews can be found in Handler (1985) and Koppitz (1968, 1984).

It is not surprising that the DAP is so popular with clinicians. The following are some key reasons for its wide acceptance:

1. The Draw-A-Person is a simple, easy task for most children, and young children especially who are more fluent nonverbally than verbally like drawing tasks and will usually cooperate.
2. The Draw-A-Person is cost efficient: It is quick and easy to administer, it is typically completed within five or ten minutes and it requires few materials. This makes it especially popular with busy clinicians.
3. In addition to being quick and easy to administer, the Draw-A-Person often yields a great deal of information concerning the child's self-concept, intellectual functioning, developmental level, personality style as well as suggesting areas of conflict.
4. The Draw-A-Person has few age and intelligence limitations.
5. As a result of the Draw-A-Person being quick and easy to administer, it lends itself well as an instrument to measure changes in psychotherapy.
6. The Draw-A-Person has no external stimulus or structure. There are no designs to copy, nor vague forms to stimulate association or sketchy drawings which have to be constructed into stories. Therefore, the clinician has the opportunity to observe the child functioning

on a relatively unstructured task; the structure must come from within. The child's functioning under this condition can be compared with functioning on more structured tasks in order to determine the degree to which the child may need external structure in order to function, as well as to determine the qualitative effects of functioning when external structure is absent.

I have found the DAP most informative when viewed from a developmental point of view. In that vein it is instructional to consider some of the requirements placed upon children when they are asked to draw a person:

1. They are required to have organizational and interpretive skills. That is, they need to be able to conceptualize the form of a human.
2. They must have sufficient ability to visualize what a human figure looks like, as they are not asked to copy a figure but to conceptualize and visualize what the figure looks like as they are provided a blank piece of paper.
3. They are called upon to use fine motor skills as they reproduce the visualized image of the person.
4. The drawing of a person has affective components that can interfere with or enhance the child's drawing. I have found it extremely helpful to obtain a sample of less affect-laden drawings, such as geometric designs, in addition to the person.

First, I consider the child from a developmental point of view and obtain a developmental age. I do not advocate obtaining an overall eyeball impression of the drawing as a starting point. The "developmental age" is the cornerstone of the assessment approach being suggested, and I do not want to introduce any unnecessary bias.

After obtaining the developmental age, I then consider whether or not a developmental lag, neurological condition, or emotional or attitudinal factors are present. A major concept that I find helpful when examining the drawings and generating hypotheses is "drawing consistency."

1. The greater the consistency of the figure drawn, the more likely it is that the obtained developmental age is accurate; with inconsistency, the child is usually capable of performing at a developmental age indicated by the more advanced implications of the drawing. For example, a child with developmental age of 5 years 6 months may succeed in a few items and miss several and then receive credit for

some advanced items. This child can be considered to be functioning closer to the developmental age associated with the successes at the higher level than to the obtained developmental age.

2. The greater the inconsistency between the geometric design and the figure, the more likely it is that problems are present. When the figure is poorer, the likelihood of emotional complications is suggested. When the geometric designs are poorer and at a younger developmental age than the figure, the possibility of a developmental delay or neurological impairment is more likely. Relatively high geometric-design performance, in contrast to low figure-drawing performance, may signal some experiential deprivation.

Hypotheses regarding the child's personality style are based upon the schema that characterizes children as too loose or too tight (see Chapter 2) and are generated from the figure drawn as well as the behavior of the child.

Requesting the child to create a story about the figure drawn or to answer specific questions about the figure, such as its age, school placement, interests, and so on, or introducing the Kinetic Family Drawing Test (Burns and Kaufman, 1980), can provide supplemental or confirmatory information about the child's feelings of esteem, self-concept, and view of his or her position in the family.

The materials required to administer the DAP are a pencil with an eraser or, in the case of some preschool children, crayons and a piece of 8½" by 11" paper. When using the DAP to gain specific information about the child, it is important that the paper be approximately 8½" by 11", as the size of the paper can influence the size of the person drawn and will then give misleading information. The child is asked to draw a person as well as he or she can possibly draw. Following the completion of the DAP, the clinician can ask projective questions regarding the figure drawn or request the child to make up a story about the picture. These are some areas of interest to most clinicians when they ask about the person drawn:

1. Sex of the figure
2. Age of the figure
3. Grade in school
4. School performance of the figure
5. Feelings the figure may be having
6. Peer and sibling relations

Most children provide rather sparse stories when left to their own devices and need assistance in the form of questions or cues.

The child is also requested to draw some geometric designs. The Bender-Gestalt Visual Motor Test, scored according to the procedure suggested by Koppitz (1975), is one approach to getting this information. However, for those not familiar with the Bender-Gestalt or not wanting to introduce a more formal testing ambiance into the play session, the following rule of thumb can be helpful: Five-year-old children are able to draw very good circles and adequate squares and triangles. Seventy-five percent of seven-year-olds are capable of drawing diamonds, and by the age of eight, children can write a series of numbers quite nicely as well as draw competent diamonds. The ten-year-old child is capable of drawing and copying complex designs, such as a diamond within a square within a circle, or overlapping all figures of a series of successively nested diamonds.

SCORING

In addition to being used as a freestanding measure of intelligence (Goodenough, 1926; Harris, 1963; Koppitz, 1968), the drawing of a human has also been included as a subtest in a number of more complex psychological tests (Stanford-Binet, 1960; McCarthy, 1972; Brenner, 1964). The major difference between the two uses of the DAP involves the number of items scored. Those that require more items scored stress motor coordination, spatial detail, proportionality, and maturity of drawing techniques.

The drawing of the human figure is not a reproductive task but a representational one. The drawing follows a developmental sequence, and it is only when the child reaches the age of 9 or 10 that the drawing of the child's mental image becomes more objective and approaches the visual image of how a person actually looks. The 2- to 4-year-old child makes drawings that usually consist of scribbles or unrecognizable, although appropriate, labeled parts. From 4 to 6 years, there is a transition, with "potato man" being among the first clearly representational figures. "Snowman" and "stickman" follow. Between the ages of 6 and 10, the drawings become progressively more intelligible and appropriate (DiLeo, 1970).

There are 15 key items that form the basis for my practical and brief scoring systems. They are presented here in a quasi-developmental order.

The items are based upon the work of Koppitz (1968) Dillard and Landsman (1968) and Bakwin, Weider, and Bakwin (1948).

The 15 items are:

1. Head present
2. Legs present
3. Arms present
4. Body present
5. Eyes present
6. Mouth present
7. Nose present
8. Length of trunk greater than breadth
9. Both legs and arms attached to trunk
10. Neck present
11. Shoulders indicated
12. Hair shown
13. Hands or fingers present
14. Arms or legs in two dimensions
15. Feet present

Some additional items that tend to appear in the drawings of older latency-aged children (9–12) are:

1. Legs are arms in two dimensions
2. Attachment of arms and legs to body at correct position
3. Mouth or nose shown in two dimensions
4. Two or more articles of clothing shown
5. Pupils drawn
6. Eye detail—brow, lash, or both
7. Ears present
8. Hair drawn so that it is better than a scribble, covers more than the circumference of the head, and the outline of the head is not visible
9. Correct number of fingers shown
10. Neck continues with shoulder

The figure is scored for the presence of each of the criteria items (the basic 15 or any of the additional 10). Every item scored results in a credit of three months, or one year for every four items present. All children start with a basal age of 3½ years. Add an additional 3½ years to the score and the sum represents the developmental age of the child. The developmental age, while correlated with intelligence, should never be interpreted as an I.Q. The greater the discrepancy between the developmental age and the chronological age, the more the child is at risk for impairment, immaturity, or delay. Discrepancies of 12 to 18 months indicate the need for a more complete evaluation. Figure 2 presents some examples of scored DAP's.

UNDERSTANDING THE DRAWING

Developmental Consistencies

1. When there is good developmental consistency within the figure itself and between the figure and the geometric design, there is greater likelihood that the obtained developmental age is valid, and those factors that the drawing taps are not contributing to the child's problems.
2. When there is inconsistency within the figure, with the overall drawing suggesting a lower developmental age than might be expected, there may be inefficiencies in performance. A more in-depth evaluation may be warranted: the child's auditory and visual discrimination abilities, attention, concentration, memory functions, and general intelligence are areas that bear further investigation.
3. When the discrepancy is between the figure and the geometric design, with the designs showing poorer performance, perceptual-motor assessment or psychoneurological testing should be obtained, along with a good developmental history.
4. When the figure drawn is poorer than the geometric design, emotional or interpersonal factors may be hindering performance and further psychological projective testing should be pursued. Hypotheses regarding interferences in functioning due to emotional difficulties or social immaturity should be considered and a social history used to rule out experiential understimulation.

When developmental immaturity is unlikely, as under conditions of figure consistency or geometric designs drawn at a higher developmental level, then the clinician can have greater confidence in inferences regarding the personality style of the child.

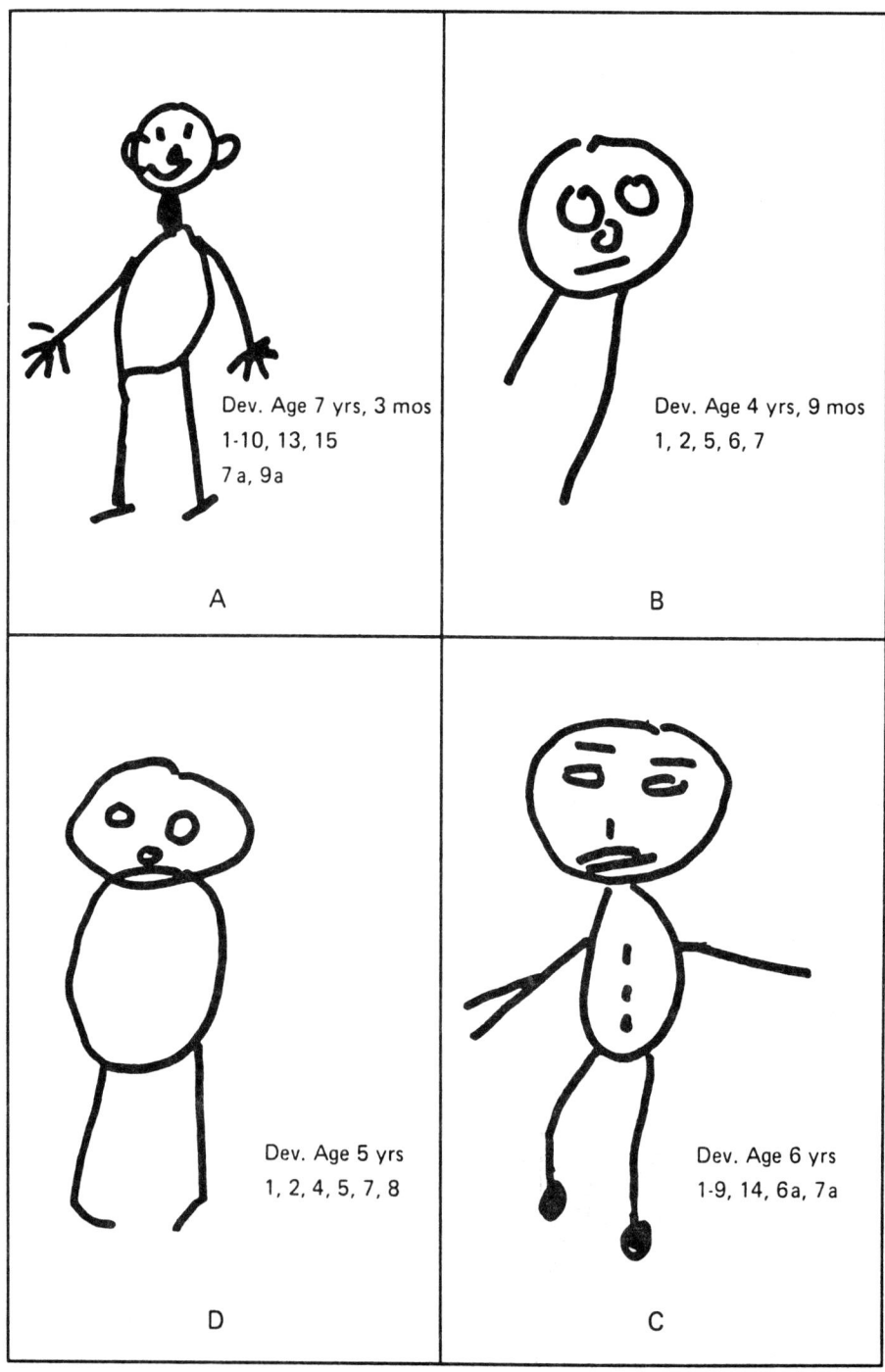

Figure 2. Examples of Scored DAPS

Personality Style

A myriad of works have suggested different signs to look for in the drawing when generating interpretive hypothesis: the content of the figure drawn, such as sex, posture, facial expression, shading; and the way in which the figure was drawn, including size, placement of the figure on the page, pressure, and line quality, have been stressed in interpretive manuals. For example, size of the figure has been related to tendencies towards inhibition or expansiveness, posture to active or passive learnings, overemphasis of eye detail to suspiciousness, buttons to immaturity, and shading to anxiety. Some signs have been based upon considerable empirical investigation and others rooted in clinical wisdom.

The DAP can be a rich source of hypotheses regarding an individual's emotional functioning, personality, and areas of conflict. A number of useful handbooks elaborate the possible DAP signs. Rather than providing a truncated list of such signs, the interested reader is referred to this rich literature (Hammer, 1958, 1968; Handler, 1985; Koppitz, 1984; Machover, 1949). It is reasonable to expect a relationship between the figure drawn and the personality style of the child. The drawing is not a copy but a representational offering of children's views of themselves based upon experiences with their environment and their significant others (peers, siblings, and parents). These experiences contribute to their self-view and, in turn, to their perceptions of their world.

The two dimensions of personality style elaborated in Chapter 2 will be indicated in the drawing of the person. The particular signs that are suggested are empirically rooted (Handler, 1985; Koppitz, 1975; Machover, 1949).

The following are the key personality style signs:

Too tight:	Too loose:
1. Tiny figures	1. Poor integration of body parts
2. Hands cut off	2. Asymmetry of limbs
3. Shading	3. Large figure
4. Omission of eyes	4. Teeth showing
5. Arms or legs together	5. Excessively long hands or excessively long arms

Most children tend to draw same-sex figures. Regardless of whether the predominant indications are that the child is too loose or too tight, if the figure drawing is of the opposite sex, then there is a good possibility that difficulties exist in sexual identification.

The Squiggle Game

The Squiggle Technique was originally introduced by Winnicott (1971) to communicate with child patients by use of metaphor. Basically, Winnicott drew a squiggle which is a variation of a straight, curved, wavy, or zigzagged line and asked the child to make it into a picture. The squiggle game as introduced by Winnicott has been modified by Claman (1980). He asked children to make the squiggle into a picture and then to tell a story about their picture. The child then makes a squiggle to which the therapist makes a picture and creates a story. Children enjoy drawing, telling and listening to stories. Squiggles are a helpful approach to gain information regarding the emotional needs of children while imparting information to them which can suggest more adaptive approaches to their problems. Gardner (1971) concludes: "Few children are interested in gaining conscience awareness of their unconscious processes, yet alone using such insights therapeutically."

The squiggle game begins by inviting the child to play the squiggle game: "Do you know what a squiggle is?" Regardless of the child's answer, tell him what a squiggle is by drawing one and then say, "A squiggle looks like this, it is just a wiggly line." Instruct the child how to play the game. "This is how we play squiggles. I make a squiggle and then you have to make it into a picture and tell a story about your picture." If so inclined, the therapist can add, "After you finish your story, you can draw a squiggle for me to make into a picture and tell a story about."

I have found that children will lose interest in the task after three to five squiggles. However, they often ask to play the game in subsequent sessions. It is often useful to use similar squiggles with children so that you begin to build an internal set of expectancies. Figure 3 presents examples of some squiggles which have been helpful in eliciting responses from children.

The clinician needs to pay attention to the accuracy between what is drawn and the verbalized label. The poorer the relationship between what is drawn and the label, the more disturbed may be the child. A preliminary study conducted at the Rochester Mental Health Center compared children with comparable I.Q. scores who were attending a day treatment program with children seen in their outpatient program. The day treatment children scored significantly lower than the outpatient population, indicating a higher level of disturbance.

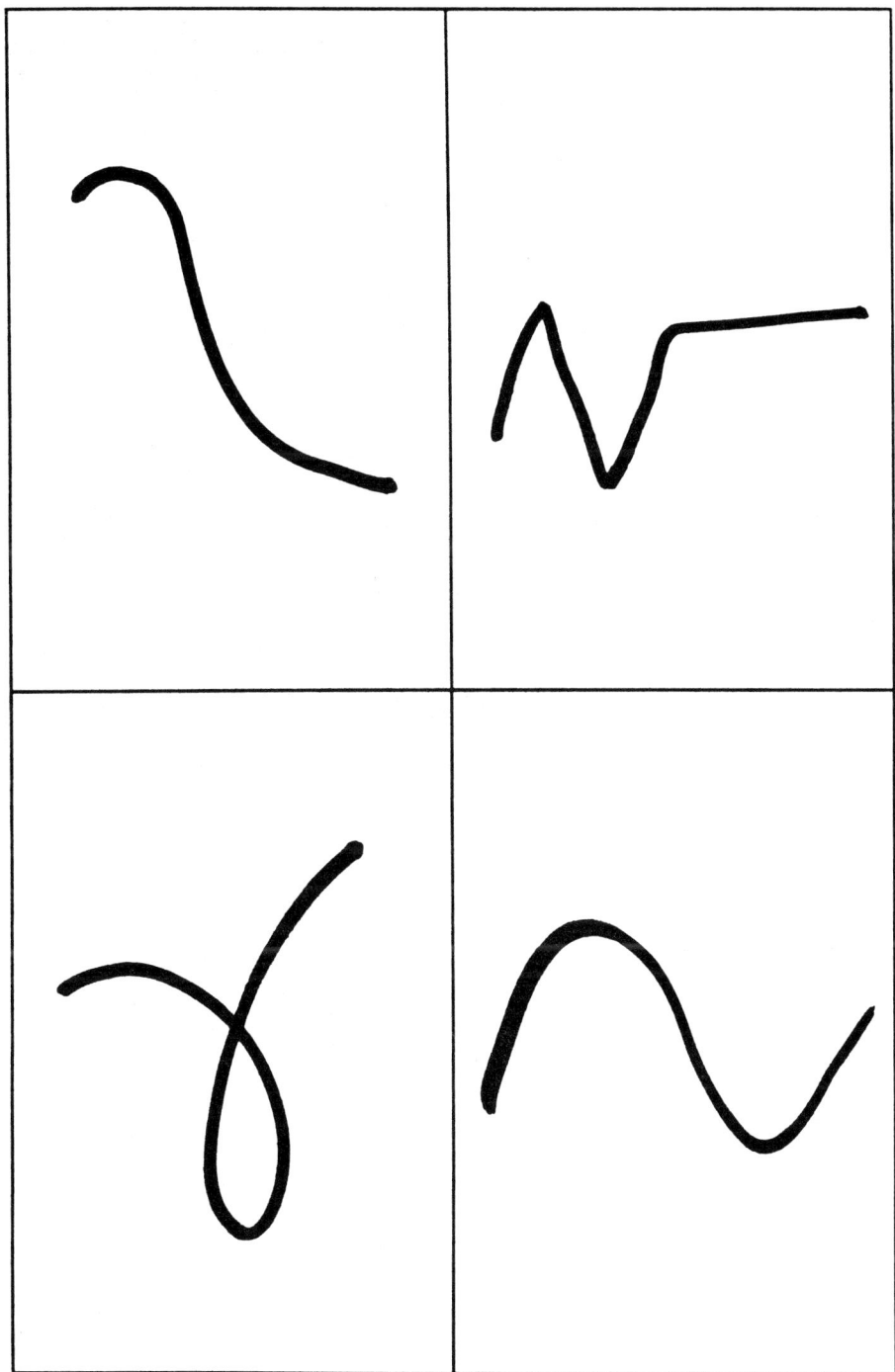

Figure 3. Suggestive Squiggles

Another dimension to consider is the degree of elaboration of the story. Some children are unable or unwilling to create a story, others will just label the picture or give a phrase which incorporates the elements of their drawing, while others will go beyond a description and create a story with the elements of a beginning, a middle and an ending.

It has been my experience that children who are loose create rather limited, disjointed stories, while those who are tight either refuse to create a story or else create lengthy, elaborate stories. The content of the story may provide insight into the child's problems and give the therapist some themes which might be included in the story told back to the child. While one picture may be worth a thousand words, the therapist's message will be elaborated in the story which is told to the child. The squiggle is one helpful way of involving the child to listen to your message, although there are others (for example, Gardner's Mutual Story-Telling Technique, 1971).

Kissel (1972), Kritzberg (1975), and Claman (1980) have introduced variations and elaborations of storytelling techniques. Kritzberg (1975) has provided a system for categorizing stories to facilitate the clinician's involvement, while Claman (1980) has children make a squiggle into a picture and then create a story about the squiggle. Kissel (1972) suggests that the child create images while listening to his or her story and also supply adaptive endings which are recorded and listened to by both therapist and child. Homework exercises then can be assigned to the child to provide added exposure to both conflict and active solutions, which also counteracts the child's attempt to avoid working on the conflict in the time away from therapy. Basically, these techniques help children discover better ways of adapting to anxiety-provoking situations without engendering too much anxiety in the child or the relationship. Furthermore, the novelty, structure, and active aspects of the procedure enhance a child's motivation. The following illustrates a storytelling technique.

A sulky, easily angered, extremely short-statured 11-year-old was the third out-of-wedlock child in a family of five. He was referred to the clinic by the local children's department of social services because the foster parents were finding him difficult to control. The child told the following story during his fifth therapy session:

> Once upon a time there was a prince and a black widow spider. The prince did not like this black widow spider so the black widow spider

said, "If you marry me, I'll give you a million dollars," and so he married her and she gave him the million dollars; and she said, "If you give me a diamond ring, I'll give you a thousand dollars," and so he gave her a diamond ring and she gave him a thousand dollars. But then the black widow spider did not like him anymore and she played a dirty trick on him. She said, "If you give me a kiss, I'll give you a billion dollars." The handsome prince kissed her and she poisoned him; then the prince died and she found another one, and she kept wandering, looking for another one because that one was no good. Then one day she met this great old goat—he was about 1 million years old—and she said, "Will you please marry me and I'll give you a thousand dollars." So the goat married her and she gave him the money, but then she did not like him anymore so she killed him, too. She poisoned him just like she did the prince; and then she met a little white polar bear who was sitting in a tree and he said, "I'll marry you on one condition. If you promise not to poison me, or I'll never marry you." And so the polar bear married her, and she said, "Okay, I'll not poison you." She did not promise but she said she would not. The next day she put arsenic in his coffee, and he said, "What's in that?" She said, "Oh, just some arsenic and soon you will die—in about 10 minutes." So the polar bear began coughing and running around yelling, "I've poisoned, let me out of here." But all the doors were locked, and he could not get out of a window because they were all locked also, and so he busted one window and climbed out and escaped and he went home. The moral of the story was never marry a poisoned lady.

I chose to focus on the child's conflict of not being able to adequately express his true wishes. The bear was interpreted as the figure who best represented the child because he was the third child and the bear, the third victim of the spider.

The story that I created duplicated the child's, except that in response to her offer of marriage, the old goat said, "I don't think so, because I am old and I don't want to get married." When the spider approached the polar bear and said, "Polar bear, marry me," the polar bear said, "I don't think I want to marry you," and the black widow spider said, "Polar bear, if you marry me, I will make you rich and give you lots of money," and the polar bear said to the black widow spider, "That's very nice of you, you must be a kind black widow spider, but I think I'd rather wait and find somebody that I really like and then get married, even though I think you're nice. Thank you for your offer and goodbye." The moral of this story was telling how you feel is better than holding it in.

When applying story-telling techniques to engage children, clinicians are faced with choosing from the number of possible choices that usually come to mind. When developing the plot, create an action story which has a beginning, middle, and especially an ending which, whenever possible, conveys an active mastery message.

Kritzberg (1975) suggests that most stories clinicians create can be categorized as mirror stories, suggestive-directive stories, or indirect-interpretive stories. Claman (1980) has found this approach helpful while using the squiggle-drawing game.

1. **Mirror stories.** In this type of story, the clinician repeats the child's story with only minor changes in plot, characters, action, outcome, and meaning (i.e. a cat can be changed to a dog, a lake to a sea). Mirror stories are effective ways of informing children that you are listening and paying attention to them as well as encouraging their self-expression. This type of story is a "safe" one to tell and can be likened to reflections or repetitions in talk therapy. The mirror story is the type of story to create when you are unable to decide upon a dynamically oriented mastery story.

2. **Suggestive-directive stories.** These stories relate to conflicts concerning general developmental-psychosocial tasks and encourage active mastery. Themes which express *trust* (don't be afraid of people), *self-expression* (talking is helpful; see example), *peer relations* (friends are fun, stand up to bullies), and *persistence* (don't be discouraged by failure) are some of the usual ones which these stories encompass. The clinician's message or parts of it are incorporated in the child's subsequent stories. If the child relates reality incidents which were handled more adaptively than in the past, then the clinician's message is being understood and assimilated.

3. **Indirect-interpretive stories.** These stories focus on a specific, current problem of a child (i.e. fear of swimming, fear of the dark, being shy, and fear of dogs). The clinician emphasizes the child's worry and uses a desensitization model with the addition of supportive elements to reduce anxiety and fear as the story unfolds.

Conquering Specific Fears With Drawing

Children who are just entering school, and early elementary age children, are often struggling with issues involving autonomy, initiative and industry. The mastering of their own body, socializing with other youngsters and how to control their emotions are extremely important for the child if the child is to develop a sense of adequacy and esteem. Skills can be acquired in learning how to manipulate variables that effect children's functioning. Indeed, the more successful children feel in controlling themselves, that is, the more they are taught certain skills which they can perform whenever they feel the twinges of anxiety burgeoning within, the more power they have over their environment and the greater increments of self-esteem and self-respect they will accrue. Thus, if children can be taught ways of mastering anxiety-stimulating situations, they will be helped to minimize self-defacing thoughts which accompany fears and also develop increments of self-esteem as they learn active mastery techniques.

Kissel (1983) and Crowley and Mills (1989) have devised some brief graphic approaches to helping young fearful and phobic children come to grips with their specific fear or worry.

Crowley and Mills instruct the child to draw their fear or worry. On a second piece of paper the child then draws their favorite cartoon character or a cartoon character they believe could be of help in solving the problem.

Finally, the third step in the procedure has the child draw a picture of how they believe the problem, fear, or worry will look when it is all better. One can vary the technique by having the child imagine how the cartoon character can help the child solve the problem or have the child ask the cartoon character in imagination to present some solutions and then see themselves attempting the solutions suggested. This technique is quite helpful with young children.

> An eight-year-old boy was frightened to go up to his room alone or down to the basement. During our second meeting which was one week prior to the Super Bowl, I discovered that John Elway was his favorite football player. I suggested that he imagine that he and John Elway were in the basement and a monster approached them and that John Elway, who was holding a football, threw it at the monster and knocked him out. I suggested he then saw himself doing the same thing with John Elway at his side. He complied with the task, in the office, but said he thought it was "silly." At our next session he reported that he was

able to go down to the basement and up to his room alone because he did as instructed. This was corroborated by parents at the time of the meeting and four weeks later.

The Erase-A-Fear game has also been used effectively by the author with young children in individual play therapy. It can also be readily adopted for small groups (Kissel, 1983).

The game begins with discussing a worry. Children tend to be less defensive talking about worries than fears. The therapist ultimately answers the question, "What's a worry?" (if the child doesn't) by saying, "A worry is when you think about something over and over again even when you don't want to." Next the therapist informs the child, "Sometimes worries are turned-in fears just as (cite child's fear) and I want to show you something a lot of boys and girls do to help them when they have a worry." Give the child a piece of paper, a pencil with an eraser, and ask him/her to complete the sentence:

I am afraid of _____.

Now erase the last word and crinkle the paper up.

Next write:

I am afraid of. Then erase "afraid of" and crinkle the paper up—Good!

Now on the next piece of paper write:

"I am" and then erase "am" and crinkle the paper up—Good!

Now, on the next piece of paper write "I."

Draw a circle around the I, add two eyes and a smiling mouth. Look at the smiling face and smile yourself.

Now when your smiling it's difficult to worry.

When you feel worried, sad, embarrassed or scared of something, try playing the feeling-eraser game and it will help reduce some of the worry. We can play the game whenever you want.

Construction Tasks

There are many types of construction activities such as leather crafts, weaving pot holders, and model building which are helpful for maneuvering with emotionally disturbed, inattentive and impulsive children.

Model building is a task well-suited for engaging children who are too loose. A 9-year-old third grader of average intelligence, with poor coordination, impulsivity, and perceptual impairment, was referred to a mental health center because of disruptive classroom behavior and poor school achievement. Initially, he was quite belligerent, often refusing to talk. He showed little awareness of the presence of different games and models in the playroom. During the third session, it was suggested that he might be interested in working on a model. The boy was provided with a few models (with a probability of completion in one session). Pieces were few, of medium size, and the instructions were mostly pictures to choose from.

His approach was characteristic of many learning-disabled and impulsively oriented children. He glued the two biggest pieces together. For the simple models, this procedure is adaptive; once "hooked," the child goes on to more difficult models. Lacking good organization skills and with limited ability to attend to details and poor frustration tolerance, the child had to repeatedly return to the beginning to insert pieces which had been left out. The first lesson learned was that working slower is faster. While his need for speed, finishing quickly, and immediate reward was recognized, he was forced by his experience to consider that things done more slowly ultimately get done more quickly. Through action rather than words, he began to learn the adaptive importance of attention to details and orderliness. Additionally, he developed a sense of accomplishment. The more difficult models also helped develop better frustration tolerance, as he had to wait two to three weeks before he could take home his completed model. Of course, the model was always found with the previous work undamaged, thus building trust in the relationship. As proficiency developed, he was required to become even more involved in the process by reading some of the instructions, relating words to numbers, and keeping a record of the sequence of completed parts. The major share of the work was done by the child, but the therapist assisted whenever necessary so that the project was a cooperative venture, and the child learned another lesson: Two heads are better than one.

Some specific goals of model building are:

1. Increase frustration tolerance
2. Build trust in the relationship
    a. by being a helper
    b. protecting model until completed
3. Teaching value of sequential thinking (cause-effect relationships)
4. Building child's self-confidence
    a. improvement in model-building skill over time
    b. reflecting on child's initial feelings of inadequacy
5. Foster generalization (see example—"Slow is faster")
6. Encourage attention to details

Although model building may appear to place greater emphasis on play than therapy, like most construction tasks, it requires specific knowledge, sensitivity and flexibility on the part of the practitioner. The role of the therapist involves several key tasks:

1. **Provide material**—models, glue, scissors, tweezers, most of the necessary materials which must be made available to the child.
2. **Establish rules**—it is better to permit the playroom rules to emerge while working on the model than to list them at the inception of the project. For example, children may want to take their models home even if incomplete; the rule **models cannot leave until completed** should be introduced at the end of the initial model-building session by emphasizing that the child can keep the model and take it home **when completed**. The need to complete one model before starting another and completing only one model per session are other usual rule-oriented encounters.
3. **Protect incomplete models**—it is extremely important that the child find his or her model intact from session to session. The therapist must protect the model from being broken by other children who visit the playroom. This can become a problem if one is sharing the playroom with a number of other practitioners.
4. **Focus the child**—guiding questions which direct children to figure out answers for themselves lead to active mastery. When children flounder or become unduly frustrated, asking them if there is anything in the model box which can help, or how they usually find out how to play new games, can lead them to discover the instructions. Helping the child to match his or her model part to the picture of it in the instructions is often enough to get a stuck child back on the track.
5. **Cooperate with the child**—although the child should do the majority of assembling the model, the therapist should help so that the project becomes a cooperative venture and not a "Walt Disney experience." Hold pieces for the child, especially when fine motor coordination may be causing problems; do some parts, if the child asks and the task is repetitive; for example, putting four wheels together in a car model. Make suggestions which can facilitate the assembly, especially as frustration mounts. It is very important to verbalize the different emotions the child might be experiencing while working on the models, such as pride, happiness, frustrations.

Also, talk about experiences the child might be having outside the playroom, at home, school, or with friends.
6. **Manage resistance** — some children become so engrossed in their model that they will hardly engage in any talk with the therapist. At such times the therapist needs to secure feedback from the significant adult about what progress is being made in order to gauge modifications that need to be introduced. Confrontation regarding the avoidance of talk and limiting the time spent during each session working on the model (e.g. half session model building, half session talk; or shifting to a different activity) can be helpful.

The introduction of models requires careful planning by the clinician. Several tips may aid the process:

1. **Display some models** — the therapist can have a few models displayed in his or her office to stimulate the child's interest. Some practitioners provide some verbal structure to children explaining how they can use their time together. Model building can be included in the orientation, or a direct suggestion can be made to the child about the model.
2. **Choose appropriate models** — it is important that the first model-building experience be successful. The model should be easy (see following table) and able to be completed in one or, at the most, two sessions.
3. **Help children get started** — managing frustration, focusing the child's attention on the instructions, emphasizing sequencing and the importance of attending to details, and managing the experience by setting appropriate rules are the primary tasks from the therapist's point of view. Completing the model so that it looks good is the primary task from the child's point of view.

Some children will choose a model that is too difficult even though you try to persuade them otherwise. Permit this to happen! When they get discouraged, encourage; when they give up and request another model, as theirs is in shambles, permit them to change and then introduce the rule: You have to finish your model before you can start another one, and once again guide them to a model within their reach.

The table below illustrates the availability of model-building kits of various degrees of difficulty.

Model-Building Kits

Complexity	*Manufacturer*
Difficult	
Large boats (hull length 20″)	Revell
Large cars (1/25 scale)	Monogram
Large planes (1/48 scale)	Monogram
Medium	
Small cars (7 and older)	Lindberg
Snap together planes, helicopters	Revell
Intermediate size boats and planes (1/720 scale)	Revell
Glue togethers—Super Heroes	
Easy	
Snap together cars	Revell
Snap together animals	Aurora
Snap together boats and planes (7 and older)	Lindberg

Criteria for more complexity:
a. Multiple pieces
b. Much reading
c. Long directions (# of steps)
d. Gluing
e. Number of sessions to complete

Cameras and Computers

Anxious and frightened children often are unable to respond accurately about their worries or to perceive themselves accurately. However, many times through procedures involving active mastery, they are able to work through their uncomfortable feelings and alter their negative self-concept. Photography, and specifically the use of instant picture-taking, can be added to our graphics armamentarium which traditionally has included techniques such as spontaneous drawings, copying, and painting. The following are some examples demonstrating how instant photography can be used to engage children, so that the anxiety fades but the print remains.

SEPARATION ANXIETY. Peggy, a 5-year-old girl who lived with her mother, father and two younger brothers, ages 2 and 1, was referred to the clinic because her mother had accused her of being an abusing child.

Peggy reportedly would hit and kick her mother until her mother began to cry. At other times, she would have extreme temper tantrums and hit and scratch herself. The mother, who was beaten many times by her husband, often witnessed by her daughter, called the clinic from a home for battered wives. Peggy was born out of wedlock when her mother was 15. About a year later, her mother married Peggy's stepfather. We recommended time-limited foster care, counseling for the mother, and play therapy for Peggy. During the evaluation, Peggy was responsive to the diagnostician, had good eye contact, was reluctant to talk about her behavior, but did enact the hostile relationships in the family in doll play. Most significant, she was quite responsive to firm limits which were set.

At the first therapy session after foster placement, Peggy met her mother in the waiting room and easily separated. However, 20 minutes after our session ended, I was called to the waiting room because the foster worker was unable to get Peggy to separate from her mother. Peggy refused to get into the car and was crying and clinging to her mother.

I attempted some soothing comments to no avail. I then asked Peggy if she would permit me to take a picture of her mother. She stopped sobbing and permitted me to take the picture. I quickly placed myself between Peggy and her mother and offered Peggy the picture as I shooed the mother away. Somewhat stunned, the girl accepted the picture and, as her mother began leaving, started to sob. I managed to get Peggy into the car and accompanied her home. She threw the picture on the floor and began sobbing. I held her, spoke comfortingly, and directed her attention to the picture of her mother, reminding her that they would see each other at the next appointment. After approximately 20 minutes, she consented to take the picture and kept looking at it. When she arrived at her foster home, she greeted the foster mother with a smile and showed the picture to her foster mother. Five sessions followed, at each of which a picture was taken. At the end of the second session, when she saw her mother outside, she asked if I might take a picture. Rather than just taking a picture of Peggy's mom, I took one of Peggy and her mother, and she took the picture and went home without a fuss.

As we began discussing the reuniting of the family, which would involve Peggy and her two brothers, I suggested that I might take a picture of all three and give this to Peggy. Six months later, I received a call from the mother, saying that all was going well. The children and mother were living in an apartment without the father. Peggy had entered kindergarten in September without incident and was doing well. While Peggy's separation fears do not necessarily indicate pathology, this case demonstrates the potential for constructively using photography with too tight children.

LIMIT SETTING. Photography was used to reinforce limit setting in psychotherapy with a 10-year-old. The approach to limit setting followed was suggested by Ginott. Briefly, when a child attempts to break a limit, his or her wish is reflected, the limit is stated, and, wherever possible, substitutes are provided. Finally, further reflection on the annoyance is provided.

Frank, who was an only child, was referred to the clinic because of fire setting. When he entered fourth grade, his parents moved from another part of the state to Rochester because his father had a job change. Both parents' families lived elsewhere and they felt out of place in Rochester, especially the mother, who had been extremely close to her family. The family had one car, and thus the mother found it difficult to get away from her garden apartment. Her request for the car often led to a fight. Frank was hyperactive, although not a learning problem. After the diagnosis was made and he was put on medication in the second grade, there were no behavioral or academic problems at school. Furthermore, he was a child who had many friends, and while he was quiet around adults and thought to be a shy child by teachers, he was outgoing, playful, and at times rambunctious with his friends. His mother said much of this had changed since they moved. He had few friends and was constantly teasing and getting into fights.

When seen for an evaluation, Frank showed many of the passive-aggressive mannerisms that underachieving, latency-aged boys exhibit. He denied he was angry about coming to therapy, minimized and denied problems, had difficulty verbalizing, and was unable to choose what to do. Often, he would sit silently. Following a number of minimally productive sessions, I introduced model building. After the second or third model, Frank became adventuresome and decided to move from relatively simple, snap-together models which he had completed quickly to a more complicated model. Near the end of the session, I reminded him that we had a few more minutes and suggested that he label the model so that when we met next time, we would be able to complete it. He informed me that he was quite capable of finishing it on his own at home. I acknowledged that but reminded him of our rule that models could be taken home when they were completed, but, until then, they remained the property of the clinic. I let him know I understood and reassured him that the model would be safe.

He became somewhat stronger in his request. I decided I would provide a substitute with the idea of deflecting some of his feelings. I told him that while he could not take the model home, he could take a picture of the model and show his friends what he was working on. I whipped out my One-Step, and quick as a flash, the camera was spitting out the picture. As the print became clearer, his annoyance faded, and at our next session, he was eager to get started. As a postscript, later when he was unable to finish a model, he smiled and said he hoped he would finish it the next session.

TERMINATION ANXIETY. Alice, the youngest in a family of two, wet the bed at night, was afraid to leave her mother to go to school, had frightening dreams, and often went into her mother's bed at night. Much of her anxiety and accompanying behavioral symptoms first occurred at the time of her parents' divorce. Traditional play therapy worked well, and as we approached the termination, many of the symptoms had subsided. Alice's mother had been supported and coached so she no longer tolerated or subtly encouraged her daughter's maladaptive behaviors. The bedwetting subsided as the relationship between mother and daughter improved. However, the girl had developed a very close relationship to me, as one might expect, and as we began discussing termination, she showed indications of regressing; sleeping was interrupted by bad dreams, occasional separation anxiety, and occasional bed-wetting. I asked her if I could take a picture of her to have, and, so that she could remember all of the good things that occurred in therapy, I wanted her to have a picture of me. She agreed and we took pictures of each other. Her mother reported that she showed her the picture and seemed to have been helped with the worries that she had been talking about regarding not being able to see her "special friend" any longer.

The computer has captured the imaginations of many children and has come to have a major influence on them. It can be used to engage difficult youngsters, especially those who tend to deny concerns regarding self-esteem conflicts. Children who are in their late latency or early adolescence (ages 11–14), especially if an early developing latency-aged child or late-developing adolescent, can be particularly difficult to engage in psychotherapy or diagnostic evaluations. These youngsters often are very much interested in computers or mechanized-type games and are ideationally oriented (concrete and formal operations).

The technique can mitigate the denial of owning problems; it can help youngsters understand how they can own a problem, how their perceptions and reactions contribute to behavioral difficulties, and how they may restructure their thinking and thus alter their feelings and actions. Essentially, the computer will be used as a tool to enhance the likelihood of engaging children and adolescents with the aim of fostering feelings of esteem. Language may be taught to counteract dysfunctional beliefs and feelings of helplessness or victimization. Such issues as being teased or picked on are common problems that children who have lost self-esteem complain about and are often a good place to begin. The child's problem can be dichotomized as environmental problems and "brain" or self-problems. The computer is then introduced in terms of showing a program that is analogous to how the brain works. The youngsters can then be helped to see why suggestions that they ignore problems in their environment have not been helpful. However, a program that involves helping them with their "brain problem" has more promise of success. Children are then taught how to cope with environmental stress by changing their self-statements and thus altering their perceptions. The materials I use consist of an Apple II microcomputer and a monitor. However, any computer and monitor can be used. The program which is used with the computer is written in the following basic language statements:

```
10 Print "I failed the test"
20 Print "I am very dumb"
30 Go to 10
Type RUN
```

The screen will begin to scroll as all the sentences run together. After a while, press "control reset" and all of the sentences will appear on the screen. The computer's scrolling is used as an analogy for "brain action." Self-statements that the child is not aware of can result in unpleasant feelings and maladaptive behaviors. The child is instructed to change the program to a more adaptive response.

```
10 Print "I failed the test"
20 Print "Everyone makes mistakes; I can learn to make fewer"
30 Go to 10
Type RUN
```

Again, the screen will scroll. Similarly, one could start a concern about being teased with the statement "They hate me," being replaced by "This is unpleasant; I hope it doesn't happen often." Initially, the program which scrolls on the screen describes an event followed by maladaptive self-statements that are then changed to adaptive self-statements. This is a way of helping the children begin to understand that they can influence the outcome of behavior. When children recognize that they own the problem, they are more capable of finding interpersonal solutions that make them feel less at the mercy of uncontrollable forces. They have more influence over what happens and with this comes better feelings about the self.

Board Games

Board games, such as checkers, Candyland, Trouble, Connect Four, are a staple of most playrooms.

There are a number of recently developed board games that are aimed at helping children develop feelings of esteem. Some of them are:

1. **Self-Esteem Game.** This game can be played by up to four players, although it is usually played in the playroom by a child and a therapist. It is appropriate for latency-aged children between 8 and 12, as adolescents may find it a bit "childish." It is a competitive game because there is a winner, but can also be played cooperatively in that the game is not over until all the players have reached "well-being," the area of the game which is the end. The focus of the game is on enhancing self-esteem by having the child's token move toward the end when cards are picked which describe self-enhancing attitudes or activities and the child's mover is moved backwards when situations which are self-demeaning are picked. (Self-Esteem Game. Creative Health Services, 230 South Francis Street, South Bend, IN 46617.)
2. **The Talking, Feeling, Doing Game.** This game is appropriate for children beyond latency age, although even very young latency-aged children can play it, as the therapist can read the cards which participants choose. The cards tell players to either answer something regarding a thought, feeling, or action. If they do what the card says, they get a chip, and the one who has the most chips at the end of the game wins. The object of the game is to accumulate as many reward chips as possible. By encouraging the child to respond, underlying psychological processes are discovered. Through the

therapist's responses, maladaptive processes can be corrected and by being somewhat self-divulging, therapists can teach different coping strategies for problems. For example, "A talking card says, make believe that something is happening that is very frightening; what is happening?" (Talking, Feeling, Doing Game. Creative Therapeutics, P.O. Box R, Cresskill, NJ 07626.)

3. **Social Security.** This is appropriate for children as young as six and has no upper limit. It is basically a communication game which touches on six major areas: ownership of problems, feelings exploration, problem solving, adaptation to change, conflict management, and values exploration. This is a non-competitive game which can continue until either the therapist or child decides to stop. Cards are drawn, one has to respond to them, and then the other player says, "What was the most recent important change in your life? What are two things you can do when you have a problem? Do you agree or disagree with this statement? Why?" Tell a child often enough that he is a brat and he will certainly become a brat. Both the child and the therapist have a chance to answer the questions, regardless of who draws the card. (Social Security, Ungame Co., Anaheim, CA.)

4. **Dealing With Feelings.** This is a card game which consists of 50 feeling cards which can be used to determine a child's knowledge about feelings, as well as a non-threatening means of communicating emotions. The feelings which are part of the Dealing With Feelings game include: angry, sad, frightened, ashamed, nervous, hate, bored, and lonely. (Dealing With Feelings, 1987; Feelings Factory, 11-B Glenwood Cooper Square, Raleigh, NC 27603.)

Some board games, especially those which are found in toy stores, can be helpful in binding a child's anxiety, working in a discussion mode about problems while playing low-level attentive games or using the style of play and interactions as the material which to focus treatment around. Some of the newer therapeutically devised games place greater or lesser creativity on the shoulders of the therapist. For example, the Talking, Feeling, and Doing game requires the therapist to spontaneously create a response to the child's comments so that the exchange is therapeutic and instructive for the child and takes into consideration the particular child's needs and problems. On the other hand, the game such as Self-Esteem mimics a traditional board game, in that the rules and responses are predetermined, but has therapeutic implications, in that advances towards winning the game are based upon prosocial and positive affirmations which the card provides to the child.

Children who are too tight engage the therapist around board games in a different manner than do too loose children. The too tight child is fearful, anxious and has considerable difficulty expressing him or herself verbally and, at times, even behaviorally. They are very fearful of letting go. Depending upon the intensity and depth of their disturbance, they will manifest their uptightness while playing in some of the following ways:

1. Being fearful of winning, they may insist that the therapist go first, or they may attempt to lose. Often they may believe that the therapist will get angry with them if they win and thus they will try hard to lose.
2. Their play will be very tenuous and cautious and they may express uncertainty about how they should play or, for example, if playing checkers, what color they want to be.
3. They may be overly compulsive regarding the rules of the game and/or evidence superstitious play such as having to touch a portion of the board before rolling the dice.
4. They may be indecisive especially when it comes to choosing a particular game.
5. The uptight child's verbalizations regarding losing may be in evidence, especially if early in the game it looks as if they are doing poorly. This is an indication with which they give up.
6. The more withdrawn uptight child will evidence less a joy in winning and unhappiness in losing.

In contrast, children who are too loose while playing games may show some of the following behavior:

1. Disorganized play. Problems following directions and rules are often suggested, as they may play games in a highly egocentric way. If it appears as if they are losing early in the game, such children may change the rules and at times do so without verbalizing that the rules are being changed.
2. Their play is very competitive, and as they seem to be winning or at the conclusion of the game there will be considerable boastfulness and also fun-making of the therapist.
3. If losing, they may not only change the rules but also cheat—subtly

or blatantly. In distinction to an uptight child who cheats to test whether or not the therapist is interested in paying attention, the too loose child often cheats because they are concerned with losing.

4. Lose interest in the game especially if they are losing and pay little attention when the therapist takes his or her turn.
5. At the conclusion of the game, if they lost, they may ruminate as to why they lost, moves they could have, should have, or might have made which would have altered the outcome of the game.

Storytelling Techniques

A time-honored technique for capturing the attention and imagination has been storytelling. Therapists have, along with educators, been making use of stories and books to help children gain an understanding of and come to grips with many stressful situations. Fassler (1978) has annotated a list of articles and books which help children cope with stress, concentrating on such topics as hospitalization, illness, death, separation experiences, moving, adoption, divorce, and birth of a new sibling. Gardner (1972, 1978) has written a number of stories which embrace reality and modify traditional fairy-tales to help children cope with stressful situations. The value and benefits a child accrues from fantasy is balanced by helping the child diminish unrealistic expectations about living, as well as toning down aggressive and primitive solutions to problems such as killing or being eaten up. In addition, Gardner constructs his fairy-tales so they neither begin with "Once upon a time," nor end with "and they lived happily ever after." For example, in his preface to fairy-tales, Gardner states, "In Hans and Greta, I used the universally absorbing theme of parent-child hostility and conflict but modified it. The children's problems are not solved by killing the witch and by the stepmother's convenient death. These are clearly unrealistic and unsuitable solutions. We cannot so readily murder those who maltreat us; nor do they so conveniently die (in fact, they often appear to have a greater longevity than those who treat us kindly). In my story, the children's hostilities are confined to self-defense. In addition, the stepmother is depicted somewhat less stereotypically. She is occasionally fun to be with. Also, the children do not come to the family's rescue by bringing home the witch's treasure. Children are really able to solve a family's problems and it is unfair to suggest that this is possible. The stories are complemented by lovely pictures which stimulate the child's imagination as the words are read.

A second set of stories written by Gardner focus on somewhat more realistic problems and are written for children of a somewhat older age. For example, he has a story called "Oliver and the Ostrich" which is used to counteract denial by encouraging children to face their problems and then *decide what to do*. A second story, "Say You're Sorry," discusses apologies which are helpful but need to be accompanied by behavioral changes when accidents occur. "Jerry and the Bullies," another story, suggests to children who are bullied how they might have handled that dilemma. Gardner also tackles lying with a story called "The Hundred-Dollar Lie," which talks about some of the internal dilemmas children can get into when they lie and the value of admitting their mistakes.

More recently, Mills and Crowley (1986) have begun to analyze how storytelling can have therapeutic effects. They suggest that it is important and creates a shared phenomenological reality by use of metaphor. This shared phenomenological reality makes it possible for the child to develop a sense of identification which contains the "transformational power of the metaphor." Through identification with the story or elements in the story, the child's sense of isolation about his or her own problem is replaced by sensing that the experience is shared. Mills and Crowley have identified the common elements which lead to developing a shared phenomenological experience by analyzing fairy-tales. Many classical fairy-tales:

1. Establish an overall theme of *metaphorical conflict* in relation to the protagonist;
2. Personify *unconscious processes* in the form of heroes or helpers (representing the protagonist abilities and resources), and villains or obstructions (representing the protagonist fears and negative beliefs);
3. Personify *parallel learning situations* in which the protagonist was successful;
4. Present a *metaphorical crisis* within a context of inevitable resolution by which the protagonist overcomes or resolves his problems;
5. *Develop a new sense of identification* for the protagonist as a result of his victorious "hero's journey";
6. Culminate with a *celebration* in which the protagonist's special worth is acknowledged. (Mills and Crowley, 1986, p. 65–66.)

They have created a series of stories which a therapist can tell and also suggest that, while the child listens to the story, he or she may want to relax and visualize some of the characters. Their stories are relatively brief and are addressed to a multitude of common child problems. The following are three examples that touch upon the problem of enuresis, self-esteem, and impulsivity.

"Sammy the Elephant and Mr. Camel" is a story to help children who are enuretic. Basically, the story is about a young elephant in a circus who is unable to help the other elephants in putting up the big tent. At the beginning of the story, elephants move big beams and buckets of water around by carrying them in their trunk. Each time Sammy the Elephant attempts to pick up a bucket of water and carry it, it falls as he could not *hold* it. As the story unfolds, he continues attempting to hold the bucket which falls and the animals in the circus make fun of him and he begins to feel sad and a failure. The animals keep yelling at him that he cannot control the water. As can be imagined, his frustration mounts day by day as he keeps trying to hold the water but is unsuccessful. There are sections of the story which show Sammy feeling ashamed, sad, and going off by himself crying and thinking that no one really cares about him.

One day when Sammy the Elephant was looking particularly sad, a camel approached him and asked if he could help. They discussed Sammy's problem and the camel began to remind Sammy of all the things that he had learned to do since he had been in the circus. There ensues a review of the multitude of tasks that he has learned such as walking, picking up grass with his trunk, etc. The camel also discusses other circus animals and how, over time, they learned to do many different things. The elephant was reminded not only of his past accomplishment but also of parallel learning situations for others that he might be able to identify with.

As the story comes to a conclusion, all the elephants are away from the circus and a fire breaks out in a section away from where the camel and the elephant are. The camel instructs the elephant in how to hold water for a long period of time successfully. He suggests that the elephant remember a happy feeling and hold onto that feeling for a long time or carrying the excitement for a long time of wondering what gift you'd be getting on a birthday. He encouraged the elephant by stating that elephants have good memories and always remember everything that is important and suggests that the elephant concentrate on remembering something important that he learned a long time ago and carry that happy memory with him now. The story concludes by Sammy holding his water until it was time to release it, putting out the fire and becoming a hero.

"Driftwood," another story, relates to establishing self-esteem. Driftwood is a story about a piece of wood like a log that felt terrible about itself. It was ridiculed and laughed at by many people because it just *didn't fit in.* The story describes the odyssey of the piece of wood from one demeaning, harrowing experience to another so that the log escapes being burnt in a fireplace, sent to a furniture factory which doesn't work out, placed on a barge to be transported as junk, and floats in water for a long time. During its long period of floating in the water, it felt as if it was going no place and that it might as well just dry up and disappear. The log falls asleep for a long time and it is awakened by the touch of a pleasant caressing hand and was taken to a warm house and given a position of distinction, as it was labeled *driftwood.* The story concludes with the piece of driftwood winning many contests, prizes and being acknowledged all over the world for its beauty and warmth.

Yet a third story was created to help children who had difficulty controlling their impulsivity.

"Rainbow, the Little Puppy" is a story about a puppy who has many colors, who lived in a loving family but who, like many puppies, was mischievous and needed to be taught many things. The story continues to describe, in terms which can be visualized, some of the problems which the puppy gets into such as eating family food, chewing shoes, having accidents and knocking things over with his tail. The story continues by describing a number of the things Rainbow enjoyed doing and culminates with his liking to play with friends. Difficulties ensue in making friends as he watches all of the other dogs running and having a good time. The other puppies finally invite him to play and he enjoys this activity as well. Now he had learned how to make friends, but he became more unruly, running and playing and not wanting to listen to his owners. He was sent to training school, and the process of obedience training is described as Rainbow runs and is stopped as he begins to experience being yanked on a chain. The story unfolds with Rainbow gradually being trained, learning to pay attention to certain words such as "heel" and "stop" and being rewarded for listening and self-control.

These metaphorical stories, as the multitude of others which can be created, are not presented to the child necessarily for discussion or analysis but are presented in the vein of directly communicating to a child's unconscious and providing them with metaphorical, indirect solutions to their problems as well as helping them begin to feel they are not alone in their struggles.

Relaxation

The Coca-Cola Company used to have a slogan: "Coke—The Pause that Refreshes." Today, we have few pauses that refresh. Benson (1975) suggests that there is an innate natural relaxation response in the body and that the following four conditions can help produce that response:

1. A quiet environment
2. A comfortable position
3. A mental device, such as thought or object, upon which to focus your attention
4. A passive attitude whereby distractions are ignored and attention remains focused on the mental device.

There are numerous techniques from progressive muscle relaxation to transcendental meditation, hypnosis, or deep-breathing exercises that are aimed at eliciting that response. Being "uptight" affects not only physiologic mechanisms, which can create physical illness, but also the mind, which does not work as sharply and thus can be more easily affected and influenced adversely.

The following exercises can help children learn techniques to lower anxiety and also put the tools for self-mastery in their hands. One exercise is a straightforward, three-step breathing exercise; the other is muscle relaxation exercise which can be executed in just sixty seconds.

The 3-Step Breathing Exercise

Begin by having the child stand with his feet approximately shoulder-width apart. Now, instruct the child to place one foot (the left if right-handed, the right if left-handed) slightly in front of the other (six inches or so). The child's feet should now be shoulder-width apart, one slightly in front of the other. Now, tell the child to let their arms hang loosely at their side. They should be limp. Bend the knees slightly, just enough to feel a little tension in the calves.

INSTRUCTIONS FOR BREATHE ONE. Inhale deeply and slowly through your mouth, and, as you do, notice how your body seems to lift up. The tension in your chest and upper body causes you to rise up almost as if you are going to be lifted off the floor. Exhale slowly again through your mouth, and, as you do, relax the muscles in your arms, legs, and shoulders. Notice the feeling of heaviness and how firm and solid your body feels as gravity pulls you down. As you exhale and relax, you begin to get centered.

INSTRUCTIONS FOR BREATHE TWO. Inhale again slowly, openly this time; as you do, try and keep the muscles in your shoulders, arms and chest relaxed. Breathe from the abdomen and let your diaphragm do the work. You will find that you are able to inhale and yet remain anchored.

Exhale slowly through your mouth and, again, notice the pleasant, solid feelings as you become even more anchored and more firmly relaxed. Your muscles in both arms, both legs and in your shoulders are completely relaxed.

INSTRUCTIONS FOR BREATHE THREE. Inhale again slowly, maintaining the relaxation that you have developed by now. Breathe from down deep rather than from up in your chest.

Exhale slowly and, as you do, let your mind and thoughts center on one spot: that place in your abdomen that is just behind your navel. Just gently attend to the feelings in your abdomen as you completely relax. That's fine. Now you are centered. Look around you. Notice the solid steady feeling. Now you are completely ready to read your environment. You are ready to respond. From this point, you may now want to shift and focus your attention as you react or perform.

Another breathing exercise which is somewhat less complicated and easier to use with younger children requires them to:

1. Take a deep breath and hold it for five seconds, and as they let the breath out, notice their body going limp or,
2. While breathing normally, count backwards slowly from 10 to 1 and watch their body become looser and more relaxed.

The 60-Second Stress-Reduction Workout

The 60-second stress-reduction workout can be mastered quickly, easily practiced two or three times a day for a week or two, and then be at the disposal of the child. Young children have been able to learn and master the technique with a minimal amount of effort and so have adolescents. Traditional systematic relaxation exercises have proved difficult for children in clinical practice; thus, I have modified the approach.

I suggest that when presenting the 60-second workout, initially you tape the directions for the child so that they can practice it at home as they did in your office.

Pull your shoulders up, as if you are trying to touch the ceiling, then arch them back, as if you are trying to have your shoulder blades touch each other. Hold this position for five seconds.

Let go of the tension and rest your shoulders comfortably back to a natural position. Stay this way for a second or two and notice how nice it feels in this position.

Repeat the exercise again for five seconds. Notice how the tension returns to your shoulders and neck. After five seconds let go of the tension.

Just relax and see how much better it feels. Enjoy this sensation for a few seconds.

While relaxing and breathing normally, take a deep breath nasally and hold it for five seconds. Notice the tension comes next to your chest.

After five seconds, expel the breath and notice how much better it feels. Attend to the nice sensation for a few seconds.

Then take a second, deep abdominal breath through your nose and hold it for another five seconds.

Exhale through your mouth and enjoy the relaxed sensation which is beginning to come over your body.

Now tighten your stomach as if someone was going to punch you in it. Hold the tension in your stomach for five seconds.

Relax and notice how much better it feels in this position. Just relax for a second or two, breathing normally and enjoying the sensation.

Tighten your stomach a second time and notice how the tension returns. Hold it for five seconds.

Then let go, just relax, and permit the relaxation to spread from your neck, to your shoulders, through your lungs, and down into the lower part of your body.

Now press down hard on the floor and tighten your legs and thighs. Hold this for about five seconds while the tension comes to the lower part of your body.

After five seconds, relax and notice how much better the lower part of your body feels in this position.

Repeat pressing down on the floor and tightening your legs and thighs for another five seconds.

Let go and notice how relaxed things are.

Close your eyes gently and imagine a peaceful scene, such as the waves of the ocean or the heat of the sun, both telling you to relax, relax. Do this for about 10 seconds.

These exercises complete the 60-second stress-reduction workout. Suggest that the child practice them at least three times daily, minimally in the morning, sometime during the afternoon, and once in the evening. If the child can find an additional few minutes, practice them five times a day. When the child gets skilled at the workout, taking a couple of deep breaths and, as the air is expelled, instruct the child to relax. This will have a tension-reducing effect, permit clearer thinking, and leave the body better prepared for whatever actions need to be taken.

The maneuvers which have been presented in this chapter are just a sampling of intervention strategies which a therapist can use to loosen an uptight child or tighten someone who is too loose, whether helping a nonverbal child become more expressive, teaching conflict-resolution tactics, or helping a child to raise their opinion of themselves. Therapists must keep in the forefront of their thoughts the fact that *strategic maneuvers acquire their potency from the relationship established with the child.*

Chapter 6

BEGINNINGS AND ENDINGS OF PLAY THERAPY: TEMPO

The focus of this section is on the tempo of play therapy. At what point does a child therapist do what he or she does when interacting with a troubled child? What is the flow of events one might expect during play therapy? When therapists grasp the tempo of therapy, they are in a better position to anticipate ploys and behaviors which may hinder the progress of the therapy, counteract them, and thus enhance the growth of the child. All forms of psychotherapy begin someplace. There is always a beginning when contact is established, and if something begins then there is an ending, planned or abrupt. What takes place between these two points is the middle phase of play therapy.

1. Initial Phase

The initial phase of play therapy is a conceptual rather than a temporal way of understanding the flow of play therapy, even though it has temporal reference points. During this phase there occurs a most challenging and exciting aspect: the initial interview. However, it is important to keep in mind that the initial phase consists of more than the initial interview.

Usually, a child's parent or parents are seen for an interview prior to the child. During this interview, the play therapist acquires some information regarding the problem, the duration and intensity of the problem, as well as developmental, school and family history. It provides the therapist with an opportunity to learn about the family milieu and begin to gain valuable information regarding interactional dynamics and verbal as well as nonverbal communication patterns between parent and child. This parent interview also provides the parents with an opportunity to think with the play therapist how the child should be instructed regarding their interview. In child agency settings, parents may be seen by a child care professional other than the one who will be seeing the child. For the most part, the information provided is applicable.

Parents are advised to talk with their child about the visit two or three days prior to the child seeing the therapist; introduce the play therapist as a doctor, if appropriate, or a man or woman whom they plan to take their child to see and whose job it is to help children with problems. The parents are instructed to talk honestly about one problem or complaint their child has spoken with them about on previous occasions and explain that they have spoken with the therapist about the problem because they have been unable to help their child with it. They are to let the child know that they have met the play therapist previously, that he or she is a friend of the child's pediatrician (if indeed this is so), and that the therapist is a friendly person. For more detailed information regarding interviewing parents, consult Greenspan (1981) and Reisman (1973).

During the first session, two aspects need to be considered: a content and an interpersonal aspect. Often, considerable information regarding the content aspects are in the therapist's possession prior to the meeting, although the therapist is concerned with the phenomenological aspect of the content: the child's perceptions and feelings. It is important that the child therapist be able to answer the following questions:

1. The child's problem(s): frequency, duration and the child's perception of the problem
2. Developmental, medical and educational history
3. Family relationships: marital, parent/child and sibling relationships
4. Peer relations
5. Attitude regarding need for help
6. Predominant affects: anxiety, depression
7. Diagnostic/dynamic formulation of the problem(s), including family contribution and strategies for interventions
8. Individual Treatment Plan, i.e. too tight, too loose, and appropriate strategies for intervention

A discussion of answers to all of these questions goes beyond the scope of this book, which has been focusing on the interaction between the play therapist and the child. Previous chapters have touched on answers to some of them. Thus, we will place emphasis on the second part of the initial meeting, namely, the interpersonal interactions between child and therapist.

Reisman (1973) suggests four major achievements which need to be accomplished during the initial phase of treatment and which are often important elements of the first interview:

1. introductions
2. moving from the waiting area into the playroom
3. establishing communication
4. establishing a contract

Whether in the quietness of a small private waiting room or a large public area in a community mental health center, a therapist leaves his office to go to the waiting area to greet the parent and child.

I find it helpful to first greet the parent and allow the parent to make the introductions. However, after a momentary pause if this does not occur, I find it helpful to introduce myself to the child: "Hello, Frank, my name is Doctor Kissel. We are going to be meeting in my office while your mother waits out here." This simple introduction tends to convey to the child that he/she is coming to see a doctor, that even though we haven't met, I have some prior knowledge, and that the child's parents will be waiting for them so they can leave the office and either return to home or to school. I refrain from using the words talking or playing so the child is not structured regarding our activity prior to entering the playroom.

However, even before entering the playroom, the clinician can gain some significant information by observing the child/parent interactions in the waiting room. The spiritual relations of child and parent, as well as whether the parent is involved with the child, reading to themselves or interacting with other adults while the child plays unsupervised with other children, can generate hypothesis regarding the child, which of course must be supplemented with additional information from succeeding interviews.

Usually, most children will leave their parent (some more reluctantly than others) and accompany the therapist to the play area. However, occasionally, children refuse to separate from their parents, either clinging to them, hiding behind them or burrowing their head in their parents' lap, crying that they do not want to go. There are a number of points of view regarding the handling of this problem in the waiting area. Some therapists advise scooping the child (especially if a young one) and carrying them to the play area while making soothing comments; others advise having both parent and child accompany them to the playroom, while others attempt an interview in the waiting area with parent and child in hopes of weaning the child from the parent. Having tried all three methods, I have found it wisest to suggest to the parent, "Let's all go to my room so that Frank can have a chance to see what it looks like." The therapist attempts to involve the child in a task, and usually, a drawing game such as squiggles or the Draw-A-Dog game, discussed in the previous chapter, can help engage the child quickly. Once the child is engaged, the parent can be advised to leave with a gesture by the therapist. It is sometimes helpful for the therapist to engage the child in a manner so that some distance may be placed between the child and the parent in the play area.

The major focus of the initial meeting with the child centers, however, around establishing communication with the child around their problems, talking and playing with them, establishing a friendly, professional and helping relationship and gaining information about the child's feelings regarding the problem(s) which brought them to your office, the feelings and attitudes they have regarding themselves, and their competencies.

It is during this initial meeting that the child will at times use some of the ploys already discussed in the modeling section to ascertain information regarding the therapist, and comparing and contrasting him or her with parents and teachers.

The more reticent the child, the more difficult it will be for them to respond to an opening gambit which questions them as to their knowledge regarding the reason for coming. Often it is easier for a child to talk about things which are more familiar such as family members, school name, location, friends, and interests, hobbies or games. Often it is helpful to convey to the child some general knowledge you have regarding why they are coming to see you and then ask for their views regarding the accuracy of your information. This is sometimes helpful with older latency-aged children (10–12) and adolescents. Once the child seems to become more relaxed as they sense the therapist's wish to be of help, areas regarding particular problems, complaints, and worries can be more directly queried. Since the therapist has information from parents (and, at times, schools and/or diagnostic tests), the focus of information gathering is best served when it is to gain problems perceived by the child's feelings and attitudes regarding their perceived problems rather than school, teacher or parents. This also helps to convey the notion that you wish to be of assistance to the child with their difficulties not necessarily with the difficulties which other adults perceive as prominent. During these first early minutes of the encounter with the child, it is important not to be too eager to provide a great deal of structure "to bind the tension" which both child and therapist experience.

Structuring the interview too soon or too much may prohibit you from learning the child's perceptions of his or her problems and ideas regarding therapy. You will also miss out on opportunities for observing how the child attempts to handle anxiety. Waiting several seconds and reflecting on the child's unsureness can be a helpful precursor to giving/gaining information about the purpose of the meetings and as other questions from the child emerge than continuing to structure the treatments—for example, if the child makes comments about time, informing him or her regarding the length of the session; or if the child asks for a toy to take home, discussing the related rule of the playroom: "Toys are for playing with in the playroom."

During this initial interview the issue of confidentiality should also be addressed. At times the child may wonder about what you will say to his parents, and there will come a time, after a few visits, where the play therapist of the child's parents may request a meeting. Parents are advised not to send notes via the child and also asked not to ask to see the therapist prior to or following a session, as this may heighten the child's concerns that the content of their visits is being conveyed to the parent. Both child and parent are informed regarding the nature of confidentiality which is not an unconditional one as might be given to adults. The child is informed basically that what they talk about is between them, and, unless the child leads the therapist to believe that he or she may be in danger of harming himself or someone else, the therapist will not convey information to the parent but will convey his/her own thoughts regarding whatever understanding has been gained about the child's difficulties. Usually, this is accepted by both parent and child. Whenever a scheduled meeting is to occur between the therapist and the child's parents, it is helpful to inform the child and discuss any aspects of the treatment which the child would like or not like his parents to be particularly aware of.

The emphasis in this early session should be on the goal of drawing the child into a therapeutic relationship, and thus the child's immediate reactions have a primary place of the therapist's interest. It is a primary goal of this early session to help the child bring to the relationship his/her own feelings and thoughts regarding their having to come to the therapist. It is during the initial phase where the therapist will have an opportunity to structure the helping relationship and to define the type of person he or she is. In addition, the child will be helped to understand directly and indirectly their task and their responsibility for solving their problem. In essence, the job of the child during the initial phase is to learn what is required and for the therapist to define his or her role in the play therapy process.

The initial phase of play therapy terminates with the forming of a therapeutic contract between the child and therapist. While the therapist will need to have a more formal meeting with the parent(s) regarding whether or not the child is to come for treatment, therapeutically it is important for the therapist to strive for an understanding with the child regarding why they are coming for therapy. Often, children have difficulties making explicit the reasons for coming and may state they like you or like playing. Accepting this is not a mistake. However, the play therapist needs to amplify that, in addition to playing and having a good time, there is a problem which he can or she can be of help in overcoming. The discussion with the child regarding a contract in therapy or the goals depends on a number of factors, including the child's age and maturity. If the child is interested in coming for "playing" and has some ability to consider an appropriate goal, then working towards defining what the goal may be is an appropriate reason for continuing the play therapy. When children suggest that they are doing better after the first or second meeting and that there is no longer a problem, then the therapist can encourage the child directly; by questions to discuss this with their parent; and/or often suggest a family conference to help with the process of defining the goal or goals of play therapy. It is important to emphasize that the goal which the child has does not have to be the same as that of a parent or teacher. Change in one area or aspect of a child's life can generate change and well-being in other areas. The reason for attempting to make explicit the purpose of the therapy is that it underlies a cooperative, working relationship between the child and the therapist. Even with reluctant children who refuse to acknowledge a goal or specific reason for treatment, who despite reluctance continue to see the therapist week after week, pose the therapist to wonder about the inconsistency between what the client says and does. Parents as well as therapists will not be able to get the extremely reluctant child to come for therapy, nor would any changes be manifested unless the child wanted parent and therapist to succeed. With a therapeutic contract worked out between the child and therapist and an agreement on the part of the parent(s) that the child should continue in treatment, therapy moves into the middle phase of treatment.

2. Middle Phase

Freud in his writings on teaching of psychoanalysis likened therapy to a chess game and commented that only the opening and closing moves can be taught. After the therapist has "passed" some of the child's initial tests and there is agreement between parent and therapist that the child will continue in psychotherapy, the therapy meetings take on a different tone. Most children, during the middle phase of psychotherapy, anticipate their weekly meeting with "their special friend" with a positive attitude. For many, it is a time away from school where they can play instead of work. The ambivalent or negative child becomes more resigned to having to go for their therapy and are less denying of their problems.

It is during this time that the therapist attempts to work through the child's particular difficulties and the child settles into repetitive play. Some children prefer to play a different game each week; others will repeat playing with the same game.

It is the therapist's task during the middle phase to keep their eyes on the problem: occasionally talking through the play; at other times talking directly with the child about their problems, attitudes and unhappiness; and helping children to discover their own talents and self-worth by suggesting different strategies of coping.

It is during this stage that the child's egocentricity, their feeling that they are the center of the universe, places the therapist under the scrutiny of the child. This scrutiny has been characterized by Reisman (1973) as testing the therapist. These are somewhat different than the role-determining tests which the child puts the therapist through during their first few meetings.

1. **The Test of Attention.** The therapist is expected to answer questions regarding lengthy accounts of stories told regarding books or T.V. programs, or during a game a child may cheat in a bold and deliberate fashion to test whether or not the therapist is paying attention to the game.
2. **The Memory Test.** A week or two after discussing a friend or incident, the child expects the therapist to recall the name of the friend or know how the incidents were discussed by the child.

When therapists spontaneously mention incidents previously discussed, children feel especially pleased, for it demonstrates that the therapist is interested in the child's experiences and furthermore suggests that the child's activities are important.

3. **The Anger-Tolerance Test.** Often a child will attempt to provoke anger in the therapist. They may taunt the therapist after winning a game, or violate a rule to see whether the therapist will lose their temper and punish them as parents, teachers, or other adults, or even themselves.

4. **The Test of Love.** A child once asked me to take him to the movies on the weekend. When it became clear that I would not take the child to the movies, the child became very angry with me and said, "If you really loved me you would take me." Similar expectations about being loved are often carried out around remembrances of birthdays and gift giving. The therapist communicates his understanding of the child's need but makes it clear that "what he has to give are not love and presents, but his understanding and wish to be of help" (Reisman, 1973, p. 180–181).

5. **The Rejection Test.** Children, especially those who are sensitive to rejection, may believe that a therapist is getting ready to terminate the visits if and when they go on vacation, take a trip or interrupt the continuity of the treatment. During the session immediately following the therapist's return, the child may behave in rejecting ways towards the therapist and suggest that treatment be terminated. It is a tactical mistake to accept the child's wish to terminate, especially if it seems to come from out of the blue, with little previous foundation for termination. Under such circumstances, it is wisest to suggest that the child think it over, discuss it with their parents and talk about it at the next session.

6. **Test of Confidence.** Children test the therapist by divulging some information, not only to see if the material finds its way back to their parents, but also to gage the reactions of the therapist: shock, outrage, surprise, indignation, or acceptance.

The main task of the middle stage of play therapy is the fostering of growth and development of the child and working towards symptom elimination.

While meeting with the child's parents may encumber confidentiality, it is imperative that the child therapist have face-to-face feedback meetings with the parent. Even when there is a tandem approach, occasional conferences with the parent are warranted. These conferences are helpful to enlist the parent's cooperation so that the therapist and family are not working at cross-purposes, to instill confidence that the problems are solvable, and, most importantly, for the therapist to gain needed feedback regarding progress so that modifications in the program can be introduced and realistic plans for termination can be made.

It is from the meetings with the parents that the therapist can better interpret signals that are being received from the child regarding termination.

3. Termination

Termination can be a very difficult time for both child and therapist. Many young children enjoy their visits in the play therapy room and feel that they are being deprived of a pleasurable experience. Some therapists become extremely attached to their patients and look forward to meeting with them. When a therapist has difficulty looking at the signals a child has been giving for termination or finds himself struggling with parents who initiate the discussions for ending the treatment as the child is doing better, it may be helpful to keep in mind that termination of therapy describes only half of the process. Just as school graduations are labelled "commencement," so might the play therapist keep in mind that ending the therapy is the beginning of new and better life phases for the child. It is the old neurotic and maladaptive patterns which are being terminated and are perhaps being replaced by new values and opportunities for satisfactions with family and friends in the external real world. Indeed, it is this philosophy which makes possible emphasizing to the child who terminates with mixed feelings that while you will miss the fun times you and the child have shared, you are pleased that the child is doing better so that the child will be able to enjoy other experiences away from the therapy room.

Parents, but even more so therapists, are often concerned that the termination may be premature in terms of preventing the reoccurrence of problems. It should be pointed out that play therapy cannot safeguard a child's psyche against future dangers. It is the nature of the developmental task that interactions occur between the child and significant others in the environment such as parents, teachers, peers and siblings. It is hoped that coping strategies and feelings of esteem are learned and carried by the child to new experiences so that anxieties will not be as intense or overwhelming. Therapists need to be prepared to terminate therapy with children even though insights into "underlying dynamics" have not been achieved nor perhaps basic conflicts still unresolved.

Some practical questions which arise regarding termination of play therapy are:

1. Whose decision is it to terminate: parent, child, or therapist? Since the contract is made between therapist, parent, and child, it is important to remind the child, especially when the impetus for termination comes from the child, that parents were involved in deciding for therapy to commence; hence, they need to be involved in the decision for it to terminate. If the decision to terminate is parent initiated, it is important to prevail upon the parent to have a terminal interview with the child so that therapy does not end abruptly. Late latency-age children (9–12) benefit at times from a family session to discuss reasons for termination in the context of gains which have been made.
2. How might termination affect the relations between parent and child without the protection of weekly therapy sessions?

Termination is a part of the play therapy and relates to the relationship the therapist has with both parent and child. When indications are for a less abrupt termination, I have found it helpful to diminish the frequency of the therapy sessions from weekly to bi-weekly or monthly for a brief period of time prior to termination, and this reduces the anxiety that either the parent or child has regarding termination.

I have also found it helpful to let both parent and child be aware of the fact that should difficulties recur (this is mostly for parent benefit) or should there be a wish to see me for an occasional visit for old-time's sake (this is for the child's benefit), then I certainly am available for a meeting or so.

The fact that the family is aware they can come back or call on the phone for advice or suggestions, or just to talk, tends to help with worry and concern and does not undermine their feelings of confidence nor suggest that the therapist is uncertain regarding the termination.

3. What are some signs children exhibit during the end of the middle phase which suggests that termination is drawing near?

One sign centers around change in the child's behavior. Some children may become more aggressive, others may talk about being bored, yet others may not want to come to sessions because of more interesting things occurring at school or in the neighborhood.

Once discussion of termination is mentioned, occasionally there will be a recapitulation of early symptoms.

Some children will verbalize that they are no longer showing maladaptive behavior at home or in school. When corroborated, this becomes another sign for considering termination. A series of studies undertaken by the author and his associates (Halpern, Halpern, Gold and Kissel, 1987; Halpern, Gold and Kissel, 1978; Kissel, 1970, 1974, Kissel, Gold and Halpern, 1983; Kissel and Reisman, 1968; Kissel, Woy and Gordon, 1973) revealed that parents perceived treatment successful when their children's symptoms are eliminated, regardless of the resolution of underlying conflicts. Furthermore, they want their child's therapist to provide them specific advice on the handling of their child, i.e. discipline strategies and tactics. Related to the elimination of symptoms may be a more spotty attendance, as the child's parents may break appointments more frequently or with greater regularity than earlier in the treatment program.

For children who come with anxiety, they report a lessening of anxiety and often appearing bolder in play and less concern regarding losing; aggressive and uncontrollable children begin to show a greater appreciation for rules in therapy with some generalization to the classroom.

Some children who have had difficulties with verbal expression are able to talk up more in therapy about not only the interactions but also external concerns and are somewhat less vague in their descriptions. Reisman (1968), using a sematic differential scale, found changes in the view the client had towards the therapist. He reported that the therapist was devalued and somewhat more realistically appraised during the course of treatment in contrast to the initial appraisal.

It is important for therapists to be aware that a return of regressive behaviors should not be necessarily viewed as a sign that the child is not ready to terminate but should be looked upon as an expected behavior during the termination process. It is important to continue to go ahead with plans for termination if many of the other signs are in evidence. Reminding the family that should old maladaptive behaviors or symptoms return or continue, the family can return for further treatment.

The decision to terminate like many other happenings in the play therapy is an emergent one. The play therapy experience for a child begins with the view that the relationship is started with the goal of its eventual termination. Play therapy with children is basically an ego-supporting treatment. As the therapy progresses and the therapist helps the child with his or her struggle to establish their identity, their individuality, and their recognition that it's alright to be dependent on others, then the therapist has completed his or her task.

REFERENCES

Axline, V. (1947). *Play Therapy*. Boston: Houghton Mifflin.
Bakwin, R. M., Weider, A., and Bakwin, H. (1948). Mental testing in children. *Journal of Pediatrics*, 33, 384–386.
Bandura, A. (1969). *Principles of Behavior Modification*. New York: Holt, Rinehart and Winston.
Benson, H. (1975). *The Relaxation Response*. New York: William Morrow.
Brenner, A. (1964). *Developmental Tests of School Readiness*. Los Angeles: Western Psychological Services.
Claman, L. (1980). The Squiggle Drawing Game in child psychotherapy. *American Journal of Psychotherapy*, 34, 414–421.
Crowley, R. T., and Mills, T. C. (1989). *Cartoon Magic*. New York: Brunner/Mazel.
Dillard, N. K., and Landsman, M. (1968). The Evanston Early Identification Scale: Predicting school problems from the human figure drawings of kindergarten children. *Journal of Clinical Psychology*, 26, 227–228.
Elkind, D. (1970). *Children and Adolescents*. New York: Oxford University Press.
Fassler, J. (1978). *Helping Children Cope*. New York: Free Press.
Freud, A. (1928). *Technic of Child Analysis*. New York: Nervous and Mental Disease Publishing Co.
Freud, A. (1965). *Normalcy and Pathology in Childhood*. New York: International Universities Press.
Gardner, R. H. (1972). *Stories About the Real World*. New York: Prentice-Hall.
Gardner, R. A. (1978). *Fairy Tales for the Real Work*. Creeksville, NJ: Creative Therapeutics.
Ginott, H. G. (1959). The theory and practice of "therapeutic intervention" in child treatment. *Journal of Consulting Psychology*, 23, 160–166.
Ginott, H. (1965). *Between Parent and Child*. New York: Macmillan.
Goldfried, M. R., and Davison, G. C. (1976). *Clinical Behavior Therapy*. New York: Holt, Rinehart and Winston.
Goodenough, F. (1962). *Measurement of Intelligence by Drawings*. New York: World Book Co.
Graziano, A. M. (1978). Behavior therapy. In B. Wollman, J. Egan and A. O. Ross (Eds.), *Handbook of Mental Disorders in Childhood and Adolescence*. Englewood Cliffs, NJ: Prentice-Hall.
Halpern, D., Halpern, W., Gold, J., and Kissel, S. (1987). A five-year outcome study

of adolescent day treatment. *American Orthopsychiatric Meeting,* Washington, D.C.

Halpern, W. I., and Kissel, S. (1976). *Human Resources for Troubled Children.* New York: Wiley-Interscience.

Halpern, W., Kissel, S., and Gold, J. (1984). Clinical effectiveness and cost benefits of children's day treatment. *The Directive Teacher, 5,* 15-19.

Hammer, E. G. (1958). *The Clinical Application of Projective Drawings.* Springfield, IL: Charles C Thomas, Publisher.

Hammer, E. F. (1968). Projective drawings. In A. Rabin (Ed.): *Projective Techniques in Personality Assessment.* New York: Springer.

Handler, L. (1985). The clinical uses of the Draw-A-Person (DAP). In C. S. Newman (Ed.), *Major Psychological Assessment Instruments.* Boston: Allyn and Bacon.

Harrington, R. G. (1954). Assessing childhood anxiety and depressive disorders. In S. J. Weaver (Ed.), *Testing Children* (Chill, pp. 161-185). Kansas City, MO: Test Corporation of America.

Harris, D. B. (1963). *The Goodenough-Harris Drawing Test.* New York: Harcourt Brace Jovanovich.

Healy, W. (1934). *Twenty-Five Years of Child Guidance.* Chicago: Institute for Juvenile Research.

Horovitz, E. G. (1983). When art therapy becomes the modality of choice. *The Arts in Psychotherapy, 10,* 23-32.

Kissel, S. (1970). Parent teachers' and therapists' evaluation of activity group therapy. *Bulletin of the Rochester Mental Health Center, 2,* 9-16.

Kissel, S. (1972). Systematic desensitization therapy with children: A case study and some suggested modifications. *Professional Psychology, 3,* 153-168.

Kissel, S. (1974). Mothers and therapist evaluate long-term and short-term child therapy. *Journal of Clinical Psychology,* 296-299.

Kissel, S. (1983). Self-talk for children. *Retwork, 2,* 8-9.

Kissel, S., Gordon, A., and Woy, R. (1973). Short-term intervention with adolescents and their parents. *American Association of Psychiatric Services for Children,* Chicago.

Kissel, S., and Reisman, J. M. (1968). Mother's evaluation of long-term services. *Bulletin of the Rochester Mental Health Center, 1,* 3-10.

Koppitz, E. M. (1968). *Psychological Evaluation of Children's Human Figure Drawings.* New York: Grune and Stratton.

Koppitz, E. M. (1975). *The Bender-Gestalt Test for Young Children.* New York: Grune and Stratton.

Koppitz, E. M. (1984). *Psychological Evaluation of Human Figure Drawings by Middle School Pupils.* New York: Grune and Stratton.

Kramer, E. (1977). Art therapy and play therapy. *American Journal of Art Therapy, 17,* 3-11.

Kritzberg, N. I. (1975). *The Structured Therapeutic Game Method of Child Analytical Psychotherapy.* Hickville, NY: Exposition Press.

Lubin, B., Wallis, R., and Paine, C. (1971). Patterns of psychological test usage in the United States. *Professional Psychology, 2,* 70-74.

Machover, K. (1949). *Personality Projection in the Drawing of the Human Figure.* Springfield, IL: Charles C Thomas, Publisher.

Mahoney, M. I. (1974). *Cognitive and Behavior Modification.* Cambridge, MA: Ballinger Publishing Co.

McCarthy, D. (1972). *Manual for the McCarthy Scales of Children's Abilities.* New York: Psychological Corp.

Meichenbaum, D. B. (1977). *Cognitive-Behavior Modification: An Integrative Approach.* New York: Plenum.

Mills, J. C., and Crowley, R. I. (1986). *Therapeutic Metaphors for Children.* New York: Brunner/Mazel.

Quay, H. C. (1972). Patterns of aggression, withdrawal and immaturity. In H. C. Quay and J. S. Werry (Eds.), *Psychopathological Disorders of Childhood.* New York: Wiley and Sons.

Reisman, J. M. (1966). *The Development of Clinical Psychology.* New York: Appleton-Century-Crofts.

Reisman, J. M. (1971). *Toward the Integration of Psychotherapy.* New York: Wiley-Interscience.

Reisman, J. M. (1973). *Principles of Psychotherapy with Children.* New York: Wiley-Interscience.

Schaefer, C. E. (1988). *Innovative Interventions in Adolescent Therapy.* New York: Wiley-Interscience.

Schaefer, C. E., and Millman, H. L. (1977). *Therapies for Children.* San Francisco: Jossey-Bass.

Schaefer, C. E., and O'Connor, K. I. (1983). *Handbook of Play Therapy.* New York: Wiley-Interscience.

Schaefer, C. E., and Reid, S. E. (1986). *Game Play.* New York: Wiley-Interscience.

Stanford-Binet Intelligence Scale. (1960). Chicago: Riverside Publishing Co.

Sundberg, N. (1961). The practice of psychological testing in clinical services in the United States. *American Psychologist, 16,* 79–83.

Winnicott, D. W. (1951). *Therapeutic Consultations in Child Psychiatry.* New York: Basic Books.

Wolpe, J. (1958). *Psychotherapy by Reciprocal Inhibition.* Palo Alto, CA: Stanford University Press.

Wolpe, J., and Lazarus, A. (1966). *Behavior Therapy Techniques.* Oxford: Pergamon Press.

INDEX

A

ADD and Story-telling, 71
Aims of Therapy, 88
Assessment, 20–23
Attentive Listening, 32
Axline, 6, 89

B

Bakwin, H., 45, 89
Bandura, 5, 89
Behavior Therapy, 4
Benson, 72, 89
Binding Anxiety, 37
Board Games, 65
Breathing Exercises, 72–73
Brenner, 45, 89

C

Cheating During Play, 25–26
Claman, 50, 53, 89
Cognitive Development, 15–18
Computer in Play, 64
Conception of Childhood, 12
Confidentiality, 27, 81–82
Confrontations, 34–35
Crowley, 40, 55, 69, 89

D

Davison, 5, 89
Dealing with Feelings, 66
Dillard, 49, 89
Divorce and Children's Thoughts, 17
Direct Suggestions, 35
Draw-A-Dog, 39

Draw-A-Person, 42–49
   Administration, 44
   Developmental Assessment, 47
   Examples, 48
   Interpretation, 47–49
   Personality Assessment, 49
   Scoring, 45–46
Drawing Away Fears, 55–56
DSM–III, 20

E

Elkind, 15, 89
Engaging Tight Children, 39–56
Emotional Development, 12–15
Enuresis and Story Telling, 70
Erase-A-Fear, 56
Erikson, 12
Eysenck, 4

F

Fassler, 68, 89
Fairy Tales, 69
Family Therapy, 5
First Meeting with Child, 78
Freud, A., 3, 20, 89
Freud, S., 3
Fromm, 13
Functions of Therapist, 8

G

Games with Loose Children, 68
Games with Uptight Children, 67
Gardner, 68, 89
Ginott, 6, 26, 89

Gold, 87
Goldfried, 5, 89
Goodenough, 42, 89
Gordon, 87, 90
Graziano, 5, 89
Greenspan, 78
Guiding Principles, 22

H

Halpern, 3, 8, 87, 89, 90
Hammer, 49, 90
Handler, 42, 49, 90
Harrington, 20, 90
Harris, 45, 90
Healy, 3, 90
Hollister, 4, 90
Horovitz, 40, 90

I

Initial Phase, 77–81
    Key Questions, 78
    Major Accomplishments, 81
Insight, 33
Interpretations, 33
Interrogative Statements, 34

K

Kissel, 3, 4, 8, 40, 52, 55, 87, 89
Koppitz, 42, 49, 90
Kramer, 40, 90
Kritzberg, 52, 90

L

Leventhal, 4
Levitt, 4
Limit Setting, 62
Limit Testing, 26–27
Love, 13–14
Lubin, 42, 90

M

Machover, 49, 91
Mahoney, 5, 91
Maneuvering by Therapist, 23

McCarthy, 45, 91
Melchenbaum, 5, 91
Middle Phase, 83–86
    Goals, 84–85
    Tests, 83–84
Mills, 40, 55, 69, 89, 91
Millman, 7, 91
Mirroring by Therapist, 23
Model Building, 56–60
    Difficulty of Models, 60
    Goals, 57
    Managing Resistance, 59
    Role of Therapist, 58
Modeling by Therapist, 23

O

O'Conner, 7, 91
Opening Gambits, 80

P

Paine, 42
Parent Interview, 78
Photography, 60
Piaget, 12
Play, 19–20
Play Materials, 22
Play Therapy Renaissance, 5–7
Playing With Children, 25
Play vs Talk, 18–19
Praising The Child, 35–36
Preparing The Child, 78
Premature Termination, 85

R

Reflective Exploration, 32
Regressive Play Tools, 38
Reid, 7, 91
Reisman, 3, 8, 28, 22, 78, 84, 91
Relaxation, 72–75
Restatement, 33
Return of Symptoms, 86
Role Model, 5

S

Safety in Playroom, 24–25
Self-esteem, 14–15
Self-esteem Game, 65
Separation From Parents, 79–80
Separation Anxiety, 61
Shaefer, 7, 91
Shared Phenomenological Experience, 70
Signs For Termination, 87
Social Security Game, 66
Squiggle Game, 38, 50–52, 85
Story Telling, 68
Sundberg, 42
Supportive Interventions, 31
Symbolic Talk, 38

T

Talking, Feeling, Doing Game, 65–66
Termination, 63, 85–87
Testing the Therapist, 29–30
Therapeutic Contract, 82
Therapeutic Stories, 71

U

Uncovering Interventions, 33

V

Verbal Labelling, 32

W

Wallis, 42
Weinberger, 4
Winnicott, 40, 50, 91
Wolpe, 4, 91
Woy, 87, 90